Michael Price

Windows 10
for Seniors

for PCs, Laptops and Touch devices

In easy steps is an imprint of In Easy Steps Limited
16 Hamilton Terrace · Holly Walk · Leamington Spa
Warwickshire · United Kingdom · CV32 4LY
www.ineasysteps.com

Notice of Liability
Every effort has been made to ensure that this book
contains accurate and current information. However, In
Easy Steps Limited and the author shall not be liable for
any loss or damage suffered by readers as a result of
any information contained herein.

Trademarks
Microsoft® and Windows® are registered trademarks
of Microsoft Corporation. All other trademarks
are acknowledged as belonging to their respective
companies.

In Easy Steps Limited supports The Forest Stewardship
Council (FSC), the leading international forest
certification organization. All our titles that are printed
on Greenpeace approved FSC certified paper carry the
FSC logo.

MIX
Paper from
responsible sources
FSC® C020837

Printed and bound in the United Kingdom

ISBN 978-1-84078-644-6

Contents

12 Networking 207

13 Security & Maintenance 219

Index 233

1 Get Windows 10

This chapter explains how Windows 10 has evolved, identifies the new features and helps you recognize what's needed to upgrade your existing computer. You can upgrade to the appropriate edition of Windows 10, and sign in to its redesigned Start menu Desktop or work in the new Tablet mode.

Don't forget

Within each Microsoft Windows release there are several editions catering for different types of users, such as Home, Pro and Enterprise (see page 16).

Hot tip

Windows RT and 8.1 RT are versions of Windows designed for tablet PCs with the ARM processor, used in cell phones, etc. These devices are now supported by Windows 10 Mobile.

Hot tip

From Windows 7 onwards, the requirements are more standardized, so there's less need for changes to processor, memory or storage specifications.

Windows 10

Windows 10 is the latest release of Microsoft Windows, the operating system for personal computers. There has been a long list of Windows releases including:

- 1995   Windows 95
- 1998   Windows 98
- 2000   Windows Me
- 2001   Windows XP
- 2003   Windows XP MCE
- 2007   Windows Vista
- 2009   Windows 7
- 2012   Windows 8 and Windows RT
- 2013   Windows 8.1 and Windows 8.1 RT
- 2014   Windows 8.1 and 8.1 RT Update 1
- 2015   Windows 10

When you buy a new computer, it is usually shipped with the latest available release of Windows. This takes advantage of the hardware features generally available at the time. Each year sees new and more powerful features being incorporated into the latest computers. In line with this, the requirements for Microsoft Windows have increased steadily. For example, the minimum and recommended amounts of system memory have increased from 4MB to 8MB in Windows 95 to 1GB to 2GB in Windows 10. There's a similar progression in terms of the processor power, the video graphics facilities and hard disk storage.

This means that your computer may need upgrading or extending in order to use a later release of Windows, especially if you want to take advantage of new capabilities such as Multitouch. To take full advantage of new features, you may need a new computer, for example a tablet PC.

Each release enhances existing features and adds new facilities. Thus, the new Windows 10 is able to support all the functions of Windows 8.1, Windows 8, Windows 7 and prior releases, often with enhancements, plus its own unique new features. This allows you to use your computer to carry out tasks that might not have been supported with previous releases of the operating system.

Which Release is Installed?

To check which release of Windows is currently installed on your system, you can look in System Properties.

1 Press WinKey + Break key in any version of Windows to display the System Properties

2 The operating system details will be shown (along with user, memory and processor information)

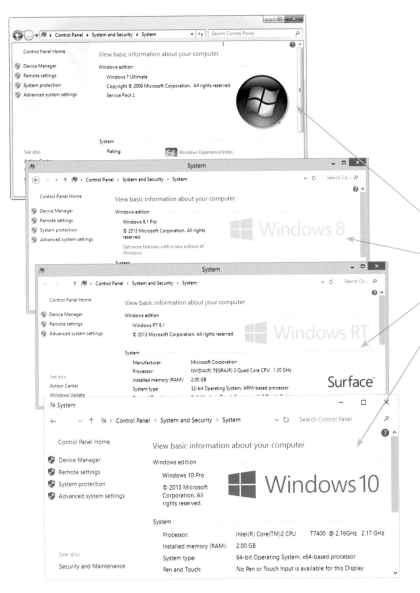

Don't forget

WinKey is normally used to represent the Windows Logo key. The Break key is normally labeled Pause/Break.

Don't forget

These images show the System Properties for computers with:

Windows 7

Windows 8.1 Pro

Windows RT 8.1

Windows 10 Pro

Hot tip

System Properties show the Windows edition and service level. Other details vary, e.g. versions after Windows 7 have no Experience Index (system rating).

Features of Windows 10

Windows 10 retains the tablet PC and touch capabilities that were introduced in Windows 8, while reintroducing the Start menu and Desktop familiar from earlier versions, along with an improved, more secure operating system with a new browser, the Cortana Personal Digital Assistant, Office functionality and other ease of use facilities. Windows 10 is also designed to run on Windows phones, small tablets, and other devices such as the Xbox One.

It will also be completely free to upgrade, for the first year at least, for systems with Windows 7 or Windows 8.1, or for Windows Phone 8.1 users.

Universal Apps

What used to be called Modern apps or Windows Store apps are now known as Universal apps, because the same code can be used to run on a variety of devices, not just PCs.

There's a new Windows Store for Windows 10, where you can download desktop programs as well as the Universal apps. These include Office for Windows apps such as Word, Excel, Outlook Mail and Calendar.

Start Menu

Windows 10 replaces the Start screen introduced in Windows 8 with a Start menu that provides a scrollable list of programs (frequently used and recently installed or all programs) in a single column, with the rest of the pane assigned to Universal app tiles. You can resize this pane or make it full-screen.

Task Switcher

To display all running apps and programs, there's a redesigned task switcher with bigger thumbnails that appears when you press Alt + Tab, or you can select Task View from the Taskbar.

Snap Assist

Since Universal apps now run in windows on the Desktop, just like programs, Split Screen view has been replaced by

Snap view where you can drag windows into the corners of the screen. You can use all four corners and have each window take up a quarter of the screen, to have four programs or apps displayed.

Multiple Desktops

When you have a number of windows active, and you don't have multiple monitors, you can put the windows on multiple virtual Desktops, to manage several projects, or to separate personal and business activities.

Tablet Mode

As an alternative for touch-enabled systems, you can change the appearance of Windows 10 by turning on Tablet mode, either via the appropriate setting or by removing or folding the keyboard on a hybrid or convertible PC.

The Taskbar is removed, and you have a full-screen Start menu that shows the tiles and hides the scrolling list of apps. All your windows switch to full-screen, or you can use Snap view with two apps displayed simultaneously.

File Explorer

File Explorer is a file management app in Windows. The Navigation bar in File Explorer now includes the new Home command and a Quick Access list of frequently visited locations and folders, plus a list of recently opened files underneath it.

Microsoft Edge Browser

Microsoft has replaced the aging Internet Explorer with the new Edge browser, with better support for web standards and faster speed. Internet Explorer is still available in Windows 10 for those websites that aren't compatible with Edge.

Cortana Personal Digital Assistant

This was introduced in the Windows Phone, and appears as a Search box on the Taskbar, with voice access. You can search the Start menu, installed apps, documents, apps from the Store, and search results from the web. Cortana also lets you speak to your PC to do simple tasks such as set reminders, book appointments, make calculations, and even identify songs!

Some features are only available in particular editions of Windows 10, or have specific hardware prerequisites.

The Windows Media Center editions (or add-ons from previous versions of Windows) are no longer supported in Windows 10.

13

The terms 32-bit and 64-bit relate to the way the processor handles memory. You'll also see the terms x86 and x64 used for 32-bit and 64-bit respectively.

14

Beware

The product functions and the graphics capabilities may vary depending on the system configuration.

What's Needed

The minimum configuration recommended by Microsoft to install and run Windows 10 is as follows:

- Processor   1GHz 32-bit or 64-bit

- System memory   1GB (32-bit) or 2GB (64-bit)

- Graphics   DirectX 9 graphics device with WDDM 1.0 driver

- Hard disk drive   16GB (32-bit) or 20GB (64-bit) free

- Optical drive   DVD/CD (for installation purposes)

- Display   SVGA monitor with 1024 x 600 or higher resolution

There may be additional requirements for some features, for example:

- Internet access for online services and features such as Windows Update

- Five point Multitouch hardware for touch functions

- A network and multiple PCs running Windows 10 for HomeGroup file and printer sharing

- An optical drive with rewriter function for DVD/CD authoring and backup function

- Trusted Platform Module (TPM) 1.2 hardware for BitLocker encryption

- USB flash drive for BitLocker To Go

- Audio output (headphones or speakers) for music and sound in Windows Media Player

If you are already running Windows 7 or Windows 8.1, your system should qualify for Windows 10. However, you must be running the latest versions of those systems: Windows 7 with Service Pack 1, or Windows 8.1 with Update 1. Windows Update will detect this automatically and add the Get Windows 10 app to the system tray, if your system is eligible.

Get Windows 10 App

If your system qualifies for an upgrade to Windows 10, the Get Windows 10 app will be displayed in the System tray on the Taskbar.

1 Right-click the icon to display the options. Select Reserve your free upgrade (or left-click the icon) to register for the upgrade

Hot tip

If your computer runs Windows 7 (SP1) or Windows 8.1 (Update 1) it is ready to upgrade to Windows 10, and Windows Update will add the appropriate icon to the system tray to allow you to register.

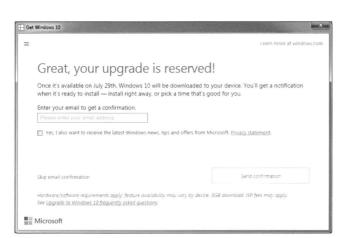

Great, your upgrade is reserved!

Once it's available on July 29th, Windows 10 will be downloaded to your device. You'll get a notification when it's ready to install — install right away, or pick a time that's good for you.

Enter your email to get a confirmation.

Please enter your email address

☐ Yes, I also want to receive the latest Windows news, tips and offers from Microsoft. Privacy statement.

Skip email confirmation   Send confirmation

Hardware/software requirements apply; feature availability may vary by device. 3GB download. ISP fees may apply.
See Upgrade to Windows 10 frequently asked questions.

■■ Microsoft

15

2 Now, the icon offers the option to Check your upgrade status

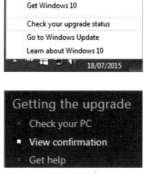

From here, you can get the latest information about the compatibility of the apps and devices on your machine.

Beware

You can upgrade from Windows 7, but you might not be able to keep all of your files, programs and settings.

✓ This PC meets system requirements

✓ Memory: Meets requirements   ✓ Data and files: Ready
✓ Processor: 1 GHz or faster   ✓ Touchscreen: Yes

ⓘ Check this report later for updates about your apps & devices. We're continuously working with partners to make more apps and devices compatible with Windows 10.

The Home edition has the Microsoft Edge browser, and apps such as Photos, Maps, Mail, Calendar, Music, and Video. It even includes Xbox One integration, to allow you to access your games libraries.

Home and Pro are available as retail packages. Pro is also available under the Volume Licensing program, intended for purchasing in bulk and is the only way to obtain the Enterprise and Education editions.

The IoT Core edition offers the futuristic prospect of remotely managing your home via Windows 10.

Windows 10 Editions

Microsoft provides seven editions of Windows 10, to suit various groups of users:

Windows 10 Home

This is for home and personal use and includes all the essential features, for desktops, laptops, tablet PCs and hybrid computers.

Windows 10 Mobile

Evolving from Windows Phone, Windows 10 Mobile provides apps equivalent to the desktop PC range, including Microsoft Office apps such as Word, Excel, and PowerPoint, for mobile phone and tablet users.

Windows 10 Pro

In addition to all the features of Windows 10 Home, this adds apps and utilities for small businesses, including Secure Boot, Device Guard, and cloud technology support. Pro is for PC enthusiasts, professionals and small business users.

Windows 10 Enterprise

Building on Windows 10 Pro, Windows 10 Enterprise adds advanced capabilities to protect devices, identities, applications and sensitive information. This edition is for medium and large organizations.

Windows 10 Education

Microsoft provides a version of Windows 10 explicitly for academic purposes. Similar in content to Windows 10 Enterprise, this is for schools, universities and students.

Windows 10 Mobile Enterprise

There is a version of Windows 10 Enterprise designed for the workplace use of smartphones, tablets and other small touch-enabled devices, providing an environment compatible with the Windows 10-based PCs in the office.

Windows 10 IoT Core

Finally, Windows 10 IoT Core will run customizable versions of Windows 10 on household appliances like smart thermostats, factory machinery, and even toasters.

Selecting your Edition

Your choice of Windows 10 edition may be predetermined by the type of equipment you are using, or by the organization you belong to.

However, if you are an individual user or a member of a small business, and you are using a desktop computer, laptop, tablet PC or hybrid PC, then you may need to look more closely at the particular options in the Home, Pro, Education and Enterprise editions. Some of the features to look at are:

Features	Home	Pro	Enterprise	Education
Customizable Start Menu	Y	Y	Y	Y
Windows Defender & Windows Firewall	Y	Y	Y	Y
Fast start with Hiberboot & InstantGo	Y	Y	Y	Y
TPM support	Y	Y	Y	Y
Battery Saver	Y	Y	Y	Y
Windows Update	Y	Y	Y	Y
Cortana Personal Digital Assistant	Y	Y	Y	Y
Windows Hello login	Y	Y	Y	Y
Virtual desktops	Y	Y	Y	Y
Snap Assist	Y	Y	Y	Y
Continuum Tablet & Desktop Modes	Y	Y	Y	Y
Microsoft Edge	Y	Y	Y	Y
Device Encryption	Y	Y	Y	Y
Easy Upgrade Home to Education	Y	-	-	Y
Easy Upgrade Pro to Enterprise	-	Y	Y	-
Group Policy Management	-	Y	Y	Y
BitLocker	-	Y	Y	Y
Remote Desktop	-	Y	Y	Y
Windows Update for Business	-	Y	Y	Y
Direct Access	-	Y	Y	Y
Windows To Go Creator	-	-	Y	Y
Start Screen Control with Group Policy	-	-	Y	Y
AppLocker	-	-	Y	Y
BranchCache	-	-	Y	Y

You can upgrade your existing system using a DVD or USB drive containing the files for the new version, or you may be able to update the existing system using Windows Update to download and install the changed files. For Windows Update, you'll need to be at the latest level i.e. Windows 7 SP1 or Windows 8.1 Update 1.

If you install directly from DVD or USB, rather than running Setup from your existing Windows, you will be unable to retain Windows settings, personal data and applications.

Upgrade to Windows 10

If you are planning to install Windows 10 on an existing computer running a previous version of Windows, you may be able to upgrade and retain your existing Windows settings, personal data and applications.

The upgrade paths available include:

- Upgrade to the Windows 10 Home edition from Windows 7 Starter, Windows 7 Home Basic or Windows 7 Home Premium editions.

- Upgrade to the Windows 10 Pro edition from Windows 7 Professional and Windows Ultimate editions.

- Upgrade to the Windows 10 Home edition from Windows 8.1 base edition.

- Upgrade to the Windows 10 Pro edition from Windows 8.1 Pro edition.

- Upgrade to the Windows 10 Enterprise edition from Windows 7 Enterprise edition.

- Upgrade to the Windows 10 Enterprise edition from Windows 8/8.1 Enterprise editions.

- Upgrade to the Windows 10 Mobile edition from Windows Phone 8.1 edition.

You won't be able to upgrade or retain Windows settings, personal data and applications if you make a move between 32-bit and 64-bit configurations, whichever edition of Windows you are using.

There is no upgrade path to Windows 10 offered for Windows 8.1 RT for the Microsoft Surface RT and similar devices. However, the Windows 8.1 RT Update 3, delivered in September 2015 via Windows Update service added some Windows 10 functionality. For example, it gave Windows 8.1 RT the capability of using a Start menu similar to that in Windows 10, in place of the Start screen. This is implemented as an option managed via Taskbar Properties.

Prepare to Install

When you receive notification that your upgrade is ready, you can upgrade your existing Windows to Windows 10, via Windows Update.

You may also install Windows 10 from a DVD, running the Setup program included on this.

In either case, you can retain the Windows settings, personal files and apps from your existing system (see page 20).

1 Follow the prompts to install Windows 10

2 Allow current updates to be added during the install

3 You'll be told of any issues or concerns that may apply to your system

If you choose not to apply current updates at this time, they can be added later via Windows Update.

In this example, there's a change of display language. However, this can be adjusted later if required, after the installation has completed.

Installing Windows 10

1 Choose to retain your existing Windows settings, personal files and apps and click Install

2 You are warned that your PC will restart several times as the installation proceeds

3 A progress report will be displayed as files are copied, features and drivers are installed, and settings are configured

4 If you are upgrading from Windows 8.1, your existing Microsoft Account will be detected

You can switch to a different Microsoft Account if you wish. With upgrades from Windows 7, you'll be asked to provide an existing Microsoft Account or create a new one.

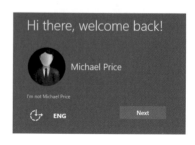

Hot tip

You need a Microsoft Account to synchronize your settings and to give you access to the Windows Store to download apps and updates. If you don't have a Microsoft Account you can create one from Accounts in the Settings app. Provide your name, email address and password, and then follow the registration process.

20

Hot tip

When there is already a PC associated with the Microsoft Account, you can choose to copy Windows apps and settings from that PC, or set up your system as a new PC.

5 As the installation continues, you'll get information updates such as details of the new apps available

New apps for the new Windows

These apps don't just come with Windows 10, they were built for it. Better yet, they'll work as beautifully on your phone and tablet as they will on your PC. Click Next to use them to open files and websites.

Photos
Photos and videos from all your devices are automatically organized into albums, enhanced to look their best, and ready to share.

Microsoft Edge
The web at its best. Take notes directly on pages, find things faster, and read distraction-free with Microsoft's new browser.

Music
Play and manage your music collection on your PC, phone, and Xbox. Want more? Subscribe and get unlimited listening to millions of tracks (where available).

Movies & TV
Rent and buy the latest movies & TV shows and watch them in high definition (where available). It plays all your personal videos, too.

Let me choose my default apps

ENG

Back   Next

Don't forget

Windows 10 has new versions of the Photos and Music apps, plus the Microsoft Edge browser that replaces Internet Explorer. There are also apps for Movies and TV. All these apps will run on your smartphone and your tablet as well as on your PC.

6 When the installation completes, you'll see the Lock screen from where you can sign in to your account

7 Click or swipe up to enter your account details (see page 28) and start a session

22:16
Monday 20 July

Don't forget

You can change the image that is displayed on the Lock screen, and even provide your own image (see page 63 for details).

21

Create a Fresh System

You can install Windows 10 from DVD to create a fresh new system on a new PC, or to completely replace the existing system on your current computer:

When Windows 10 is installed from DVD on to an existing system, you will lose the current data files and settings.

1 Setup proceeds to copy files, and then installs features and updates

2 You may be asked to provide the product key required to activate your copy of Windows 10

You need to identify company PCs as such, so that they can be set up to access the resources of your organization.

3 Identify your PC as a personal system, or a company machine provided to you for business purposes

4 Provide your Microsoft Account email address and password, or choose to create a new account

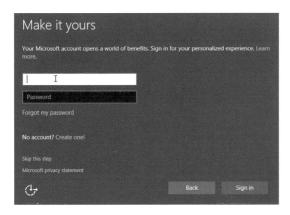

You can Skip this step, and start off with a Local Account that won't have access to the Windows Store.

5 You can set up a four digit PIN code to use as an alternative to your account password

A Personal Identification Number (PIN) code is faster to use, yet even more secure than your password.

6 If you are connected to your home or work network, you should choose to make the PC discoverable by other PCs on the network

Do not allow your PC to be discoverable if you are setting it up on a public network such as at a library or airport location.

Your Windows Apps

When you start Windows 10, you can see the apps and programs that are provided. These vary, depending on the type of Windows 10 installation.

1 From the Lock screen, sign in using your PIN code or password (see page 28-29) to display the Desktop

2 On the Desktop, click the Start button at the left of the Taskbar (or press or tap the WinKey)

3 The Windows 10 Start menu displays the Most Used and Recently Added apps and programs, plus a panel of app tiles, like the Windows 8/8.1 Start screen

...cont'd

4 Click All Apps, to display the full alphabetic list of apps and programs

5 Scroll the list to view the remaining entries

6 On a tablet PC or on a hybrid PC with the keyboard detached or folded, the Start menu will display in full-screen Tablet mode

Entries with a Folder icon expand when you click them, and contain groups of items, for example:

Click Back to redisplay the Most Used list.

Tablet mode also features the All Apps button, but it is normally hidden. To reveal it, press the button at the top left corner and display the Most Used/Recently Added list.

Closing Windows 10

When you finish working with Windows 10, you'll want to Shut down or Sign out.

Hot tip

If supported by your hardware, you will also be offered the option to put the PC to Sleep.

Sign out	Sleep
Sleep	Shut down
Shut down	Restart
Restart	

You can use Sleep when you're going to be away from your battery-powered PC for a while. It uses very little power, and when you return and touch the screen or move the mouse, the PC starts up quickly, and you're back to where you left off.

Don't forget

You can also press Alt + F4 to display the Shut down dialog and select an action.

1 As with Windows 8.1, you can right-click the Start button and select Shut down or sign out, then choose the required option

2 On the Start menu click the Power button to select Shut down or Restart

3 The Power button menu is also available in Tablet mode

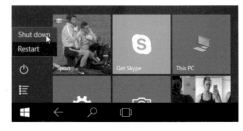

2 Windows 10 Interface

Windows 10 uses the tile-based interface first seen in Windows 8. It is designed for touch operation, while still supporting keyboard and mouse, and features a new form of Start menu and new ways to arrange and manage windows.

Start Windows 10

Switch on your computer to start up the operating system. The stages are as follows:

1 A simple Windows logo is displayed, with a rotating cursor to show that the system is being loaded

2 After a while, the Lock screen is displayed

3 Press any key, click a mouse button, or sweep up on a touchscreen monitor, to display the user Log on screen

Hot tip

The start-up time depends on the configuration of your computer and how it was previously closed down, but usually it is less than a minute.

Hot tip

This is the default Lock screen image, but you can choose another image from the Picture library, or even play a slideshow.

4 Type the password and click the arrow (or press the Enter key)

5 The Welcome message is displayed while the user account settings are being applied

6 The Windows 10 Desktop screen is displayed, showing the image associated with your account

If there are multiple user accounts, you may need to select the required account before signing in (see page 31).

An error message is displayed if you mistype the password.

That password is incorrect. Make sure you're Microsoft account. You can always reset it at account.live.com/password/reset.

If you have Tablet mode enabled on your system, it may go straight to the Start menu display.

PIN Code Sign-in

If you specified a PIN code during install (see page 23), or added one later using Settings (see page 76) you can sign in using this.

Sign-in options may also include the Picture password option (see page 74) if you have defined one for your account.

1 The Sign-in screen will request the PIN code

Windows remembers the last Sign-in option used, and presents that option the next time you sign in to that account.

2 To revert to the Password, select Sign-in options and click the Password button

3 To sign in with the PIN code, just type the four digits – there is no arrow to click and no need to press Enter

4 The Desktop (or Start menu if Tablet mode is enabled) will be displayed

Multiple User Accounts

1 If you want a different account from the one selected, click the required account in the list

If there is more than one user account, the Sign-in screen will display the last used account, along with the list of available accounts.

2 Enter the password to sign in to the selected account

3 The Welcome message is displayed while the account details are being loaded

Where there's no email address shown for an account in the list, you'll know it is a Local Account rather than a Microsoft Account, and so cannot be used to download content from the Microsoft Store.

4 The Desktop screen or the Tablet mode panel will be displayed, as appropriate for the selected device

As this example shows, both Classic apps and Universal apps run in windows on the Desktop.

Desktop Layout

The standard PC with mouse and keyboard, without Tablet mode enabled, starts with the Desktop screen. This is similar to the display from earlier versions of Windows, with Desktop icons, the Taskbar with Start button, Shortcuts, and Taskbar icons.

Desktop Universal Classic
Icon App App Background

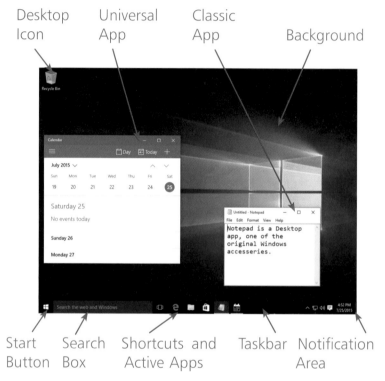

Notepad is a Desktop app, one of the original Windows accesseries.

Start Search Shortcuts and Taskbar Notification
Button Box Active Apps   Area

In previous versions of Windows, the Notification Area was known as the System Tray. The Action Center displayed from here includes features that were on the Windows 8/8.1 Charms bar.

Click the Action Center icon in the Notification area to display the Action Center. This is a full-height bar on the right of the screen. It contains a set of Quick Actions for toggling functions on or off. You can enable Tablet mode for example, or Connect to a network. There's also a shortcut to Settings. Above these Quick Actions, details of any Notifications will be displayed.

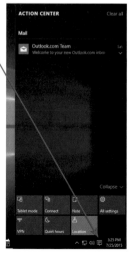

...cont'd

Click the Start button to display the Start menu, a merger of the features of the Start menu and the Start screen from previous versions of Windows.

Most Used   Recently Added   App Group   Live Tile

All Apps   Shortcuts and Active Apps   Action Center Button

1 Click All Apps to see the full set of apps on your system (see page 123)

2 Click the > next to File Explorer to Show jump list, from where you get quick access to parts of the file system

3 The full Taskbar is shown with the Start menu

The Taskbar includes the Start button, the Search box, shortcuts, active apps and the Notification area, from where you can access the Action Center

Hot tip

You can click and drag the edges of the Start menu panel to change the size of the panel and the number of tiles displayed.

Don't forget

To clear the Start menu and re-display the Desktop, click the Start button (or press WinKey).

Tablet Mode Layout

A tablet PC, or a hybrid PC with the keyboard removed or folded, will start up in Tablet mode with the full-screen version of the Start menu.

Hot tip

Windows 10 includes Continuum technology, which allows your system to transition between states manually or automatically e.g. from using a keyboard, to touchscreen when you remove or fold the keyboard on a hybrid PC.

Display Most Used and Recently Added

App Group

Live Tile

All Apps

Power Options

Back, Search and Task View

Notification Area

1 Click All Apps to see the full set of apps. There's also a button to show Most Used and Recently Added

The Taskbar is abbreviated, with just the Start, Back, Search and Task View buttons plus the Notifications area, but no shortcuts or active apps. You can enable the full Taskbar via Settings, if you wish.

You can enable and disable Tablet mode on any PC, via Settings, or by using the Tablet mode toggle displayed on the Action Center.

Don't forget

If you have multiple monitors defined on your PC, then Tablet mode is disabled and cannot be activated until you revert to a single monitor.

...cont'd

To enable, configure or disable Tablet mode:

1 Select Settings from the Start menu, or All settings from the Action Center

2 Select the System entry

Hot tip

If Tablet mode is already enabled, you'll need to display the Most Used list to find the Settings entry.

3 Select the Tablet mode entry and review the settings

Don't forget

When Tablet mode is turned on, all apps (Classic and Universal apps), will run full-screen.

- Turn Tablet mode On or Off

- Specify the action to be taken when you sign in

- Control how automatic switching takes place

- Hide or Show App icons

Power User Menu

There's a menu of useful shortcuts associated with the Start button (at the left of the Taskbar).

1 Right-click the Start button to display the menu

2 Alternatively, press WinKey + X to display that same menu

This allows you to access a set of functions that is often needed by the more advanced user, which includes System Properties, Device Manager, Disk Management, Command Prompt, Task Manager, Control Panel and Run.

Select Shut down or sign out, and you can choose to Sign out, Shut down or Restart your system.

Make sure that it's the Start button that you right-click or you'll get the right-click action associated with the area you click. On the Desktop, for example, you might get the Screen menu. On the Taskbar, you'll get a menu with related options including Toolbars, Task Manager and Properties. This displays the Taskbar and Start menu Properties:

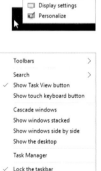

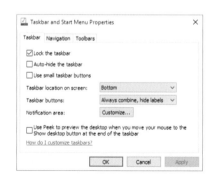

Moving Around

You can explore the contents of the Start menu in the right-hand tiled area to see which of the apps on your system have been pinned to the Start menu. If there are some apps off-screen, use the scroll bar that appears at the right of the panel when you move the mouse. The tiled area also slides vertically when you roll the mouse wheel up or down.

With a Multitouch monitor or tablet PC, in Desktop or Tablet mode, you simply drag the screen up or down as necessary to display other tiles and groups of tiles.

There's also a scroll bar displayed when you move the mouse over the tiled area of the Start menu in Tablet mode. You can also slide the area vertically with the mouse wheel, if you have a mouse connected to your tablet PC.

With a desktop PC, in Tablet mode you can also use the four keyboard arrows to navigate through the app tiles, to locate the one you want.

37

Start an App

Universal apps can be represented on the Start menu by Static tiles or by Live tiles, which display dynamic information from the associated apps, even when they are not running.

Hot tip

With a Windows 10 touchscreen or tablet, tap the tile to start the app. With the keyboard, navigate to the required tile using arrow keys and then press Enter.

1 To start an app, move the mouse pointer over the tile for the desired app and left-click to load it

Don't forget

You may be prompted to enter information, for example to specify the default location for the Weather app to use.

2 This example uses Tablet mode, so the app loads full-screen with weather details for the default location

3 Switch back to the Start menu and choose another Universal app, for example select Finance

4 In Tablet mode, this app would open full-screen, overlaying the previous app

In the example on the following page, Tablet mode has been disabled, so the selected app opens as a window on the Desktop rather than full-screen.

When you have several active apps, the Snap option will allow you to display up to four apps on the screen (see page 40).

When you have several apps running, you can show all the active apps and choose the one to work with next.

1 Click the Task View button (or press WinKey + Tab) to show all the apps, and click on the required app

These methods of selecting apps work with both Desktop and Tablet mode.

2 Alternatively, hold down Alt and tap the Tab key until the app you want is selected, then release Alt

Snap Apps

Universal apps and Classic apps can be arranged using the Windows 10 Snap feature. You can display up to four apps.

1 Open several apps as windows on the Desktop (or as full-screen apps in Tablet mode)

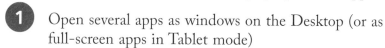

2 Click the Title bar on one app and drag it to the side of the screen, and release the mouse button when a frame appears showing the new location

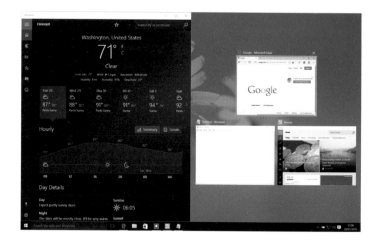

3 The other apps are displayed in Task View style on the other half of the screen

The minimum screen resolution to use the Windows 10 Snap feature is 1024 x 768, but it is more effective at higher resolutions.

In Tablet mode, move the mouse pointer to the top of the screen to reveal the app Title bar, then click and drag this to the side.

On a touchscreen, drag the top edge down to reveal the Title bar.

You can select an app and press WinKey + Left or WinKey + Right to split the screen, then select the second app for the other half.

...cont'd

4 With two apps displayed, click and drag their edges to vary the proportion of the screen each app uses

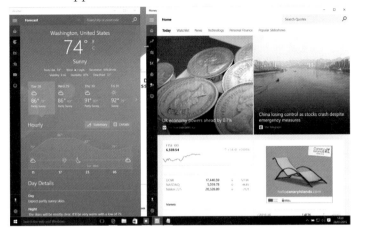

In Tablet mode, there's a divider between the two apps. Click and drag this bar to widen one app (and narrow the other).

5 To arrange four apps on the screen, click on the Title bar of an app and drag it to a corner, and repeat for up to three more apps

If you have a dual monitor system, you can have sets of two or more apps displayed on each monitor.

6 You can position apps in corners using the keyboard. Press WinKey + Up arrow, then WinKey + Left arrow for the upper left quadrant. Use Up + Right, Down + Left, and Down + Right combinations for the other quadrants

41

Close Apps

When apps are running in Desktop mode, they are windowed, and feature the Title bar with a Close button.

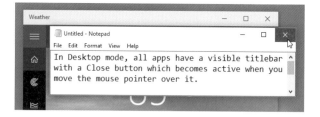

In Tablet mode, all apps run full-screen (except when Snap is in effect). Classic apps still show the Title bar and Close button.

For Universal apps in Tablet mode, you need to reveal the Title bar and its Close button (see the Hot Tip on page 40), in order to end the app.

Alternatively, move the pointer over the icon until the thumbnail appears, the click the Close button.

You can also close any app in any mode by selecting the app and then pressing Alt + F4. Another option is to click and drag (or touch and swipe) the app screen down until it shrinks and moves down to the bottom of the screen, then release.

3 Windows 10 Desktop

Although the Start menu now features tiles, and touchscreen PCs run in Tablet mode, Windows 10 still supports the windowed Desktop environment, including the Taskbar, Notification area, and the familiar windows structure, menus and dialogs for managing Desktop applications.

Desktop Mode

Switch on your computer to start up Windows 10 and display the Lock screen (see page 28), and then sign in to your user account. In most cases the system will start up in Desktop mode, with no Start menu displayed.

The appearance of your Desktop will vary, depending on configuration and personalization, but you should find:

Hot tip

You can have an app added to your Startup folder, so that the Desktop displays with that app open when you sign-in, or you can just select the app from the Start menu.

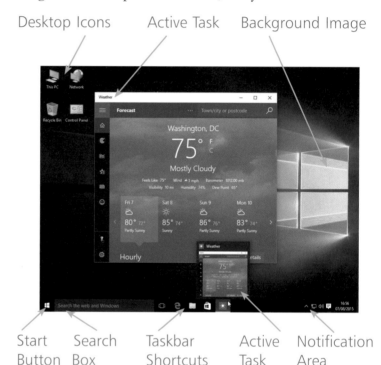

Desktop Icons   Active Task   Background Image

Start   Search   Taskbar   Active   Notification
Button   Box   Shortcuts Task   Area

Don't forget

Touch-enabled PCs may start up in Tablet mode with the Start menu displayed full-screen and no Desktop. However, these systems can also be set to start up in, or switch to Desktop mode.

The Touch keyboard button appears on the Taskbar for computers with touch-enabled monitors attached.

Touch keyboard   Touch keyboard button

In Windows 10, all apps run on the Desktop; Universal as well as Classic Windows apps. To see how these appear:

1 Start a number of apps from the Start menu (see page 38) including, for example, some Office apps

Hot tip

Right-click the Taskbar and select Cascade windows, so you can see the headers of all the open apps.

If you have numerous apps open at once, you can organize them onto separate Desktops:

2 Select the Task View button, click New Desktop, then move some apps from Desktop 1 to Desktop 2

Hot tip

Right-click an app in Task View, click Move and choose the Desktop (or drag and drop the app).

The Taskbar and Task View will now show the apps that are on the selected Desktop.

Taskbar

The contents of the Taskbar change dynamically to reflect the activities that are taking place on your Desktop.

Hot tip

Select the Search box to find apps, files and web pages.

If your PC is equipped, you can use Cortana and voice input for searches. See pages 220-221.

Taskbar Shortcuts

At the left of the Taskbar is the Start button, Search box, Task view and App shortcuts that turn into Task buttons (see below) when you run the apps – Microsoft Edge, File Explorer and the Windows Store, plus those you pin here.

Task Buttons (App Icons)

There is a Task button for each active task. The selected, or foreground task, in this case the Photos app, is shown emphasized. The blue underscore indicates activity:

One window – foreground, background

Two plus windows – foreground, background

Notification Area

The right-hand portion of the Taskbar is the Notification Area, and contains Network, Speaker, Touch keyboard, Action Center and Date/Time. These are all system functions that are loaded automatically as Windows starts.

If there is more than one input language set on your system, there's a Language icon which lists the languages installed and allows you to switch.

Don't forget

Click the button to show hidden icons, in this case for Safely Remove Hardware and OneDrive.

Tablet Mode Taskbar

The Tablet mode Taskbar is similar, but the Task buttons are not displayed. To show them, right-click the Taskbar and select Show app icons.

...cont'd

If you start more tasks, the Taskbar may become full. Scrolling arrows will then be added to let you search for a specific task.

You can resize the Taskbar to show more apps, but first you may need to unlock it.

1 Right-click the Taskbar and, if there's a check next to Lock the taskbar, click that entry to remove the check and Unlock the taskbar

Taskbar Properties (see page 48) gives options for customizing the location, operation and appearance of the Taskbar.

2 Move the mouse over the edge of the Taskbar until the pointer becomes a double-headed arrow, then drag the border up or down to resize the Taskbar

3 You can lock the Taskbar at the new size – reselect the Lock the taskbar option from the Taskbar right-click menu

You can also add other toolbars to the Taskbar:

1 Right-click an empty part of the Taskbar and select Toolbars

2 Select a toolbar and a tick will be added, and the toolbar will be displayed on the Taskbar. Reselect a toolbar to remove it

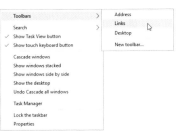

This right-click menu is also used to arrange windows or to display the Taskbar Properties.

47

Taskbar Properties

To make changes to the Taskbar settings:

1 Right-click an empty part of the Taskbar and select Properties from the menu

2 Click the Taskbar tab for Taskbar Properties

3 You can lock and unlock the Taskbar from Properties as well as from the right-click menu (see page 47)

4 Click the box labeled Auto-hide the taskbar, to make the full area of the screen available to app windows

5 It reappears when you move the mouse to the part of the screen where the Taskbar should be located

You can also Auto-hide the Taskbar in Tablet mode.

...cont'd

Small Taskbar Buttons

1 In Taskbar Properties, click the box Use small taskbar buttons, so you can fit more items onto the Taskbar

Taskbar Location

1 Click the bar labeled Taskbar location on screen, to display the drop-down menu and replace the default location e.g. Bottom with Top

Combine Taskbar Buttons

The default in Windows 10 is to show the Taskbar buttons without labels and to combine windows of the same type. However, you can keep things more separate.

1 Click the bar for Taskbar buttons to display the drop-down menu, and select Combine when taskbar is full, to also show the task labels

2 Task labels may get truncated, and multiple tasks for a particular app may be combined on one button

3 With Never combine, task labels may be truncated or dropped, and Taskbar scrolling may be used

If the Taskbar is Locked, there is no need to Unlock the Taskbar when you want to change the size or its location on the screen.

49

This style of Taskbar works best on higher resolution screens or with smaller numbers of active tasks.

Notification Area

The Notification Area (previously called the System Tray) is at the right-hand side of the Taskbar. Some icons will appear by default and installed programs may add icons. To control what is shown:

1 Click Customize, next to the Notification Area in the Taskbar Properties (see image in Step 1 on page 48)

Notification area

Customize...

2 Choose Select which icons appear on the taskbar, and Always show all icons in the notification area, or set icons on or off individually

3 In the menu in Step 1, choose Turn system icons on or off, and set each icon as desired

4 Scroll down to review the settings for Notifications

5 Choose the Notifications from the system, and from apps that you want to see on your system

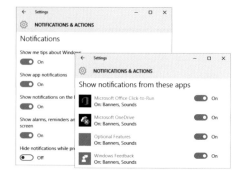

Peek At or Show Desktop

On the Taskbar to the right of the Notification Area is the Show Desktop button. Starting with several open windows:

Peek is active only when you select the option Use Peek to preview, from the Taskbar Properties (see page 48).

 Use Peek to preview the desktop when you move your mouse to the Show desktop button at the end of the taskbar

1 Hover over the Show Desktop button to see the Desktop, icons and outlines of all open windows

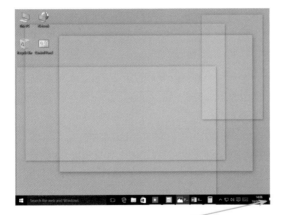

The Desktop and the outlines are displayed only temporarily, and the original window contents are redisplayed as soon as the mouse moves away from the Show Desktop button.

2 Click the Show Desktop button to hide the windows (and outlines) and show only the Desktop and icons

The Desktop is fully cleared, allowing you, if desired, to select a Desktop icon. Click the Show Desktop button again to restore the open windows.

Desktop Icons

Shortcuts to standard Windows applications can be stored on the Desktop. To start with, there are standard system icons:

1 To display or resize icons on the Desktop, right-click an empty part of the Desktop and select View

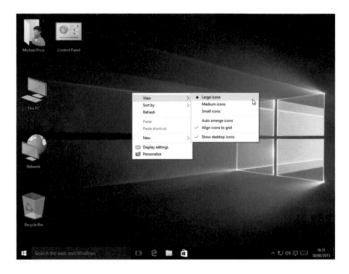

Don't forget

You can change the Desktop icons from the default size Medium, to Large as shown here, or to Small.

2 If the entry Show desktop icons is not already selected (ticked) then click to enable it

3 To specify which system icons to display, select Personalize from the right-click menu, and then Themes, Desktop icon settings

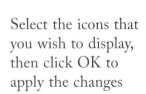

Don't forget

Click the Change Icon button to select alternative images for any of the system icons. Click Restore Default to revert to the original images.

4 Select the icons that you wish to display, then click OK to apply the changes

...cont'd

For quick access, you can add shortcuts to the Taskbar for both Classic and Universal apps:

1 Select the Search box on the Taskbar or Start menu and type an app name, e.g. Notepad

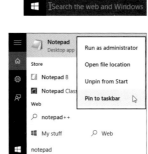

2 Right-click the result to display the context menu and select Pin to taskbar

3 View the Taskbar and you'll see a new shortcut for the app

You can now run the app from the Taskbar. However, if you prefer, you can create the app shortcut on the Desktop, where there's more room for such shortcuts.

1 Right-click the search result as above, and select Open file location

2 File Explorer opens with the app file selected

3 Right-click the file and select Create shortcut

4 Confirm that the shortcut is to be placed on the Desktop

5 You can now run that app from the Desktop by double-clicking the shortcut icon

You can also right-click the entry for the app in the All Apps list and select Pin to taskbar.

Similarly, you can use All Apps to Open file location for the app.

Open file location appears only for Classic apps. You need to use the Drag & Drop method (see page 54) for Universal app shortcuts.

...cont'd

You can also create shortcuts on the Desktop using Drag & Drop from the All Apps list, for both Classic and Universal apps.

You can right-click the Taskbar shortcut for any app you've now added to the Desktop, and select Unpin this program from taskbar to remove the app.

1 Scroll to an app in the All Apps list, for example the Character Map in Windows Accessories

2 Select and drag the App Icon onto the Desktop, and release it when the Link flag appears

3 Similarly, scroll to a Universal app such as Weather, and Drag & Drop it onto the Desktop

You can add other Windows accessories such as Paint, applications such as Word and Excel from the Microsoft Office suite, and Universal apps such as Money.

Hot tip

You may also find that some applications automatically get shortcuts added to the Desktop when installed, for example, Adobe Reader.

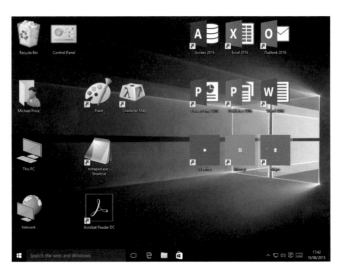

You can drag the Desktop shortcut icons to arrange them in groups, according to type, perhaps, or by project or activity.

Note that Universal app shortcuts do not display live updates, as featured with the app tiles on the Start menu.

Window Structure

When you open a folder, or start a Windows function or application program on the Desktop, it appears as a window that can be moved and resized. For example:

 1 Click the File Explorer shortcut icon on the Taskbar

Not all the Windows applications use the ribbon style. See page 56 for Notepad, an example of a conventional window.

Features of the Window

Quick Access Toolbar

Forward and Back Arrows

Ribbon

Minimize and Maximize Buttons

Close Button

Command Bar

Search Box

Address Bar

Contents Pane

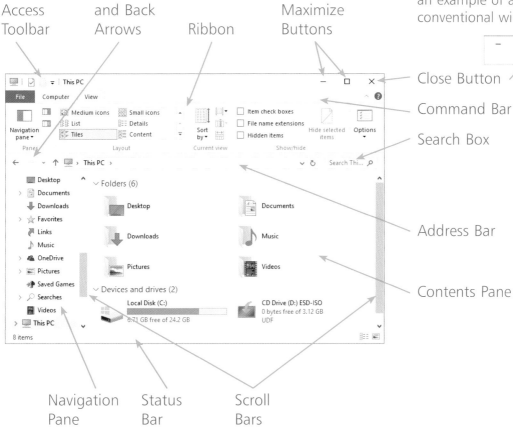

Navigation Pane

Status Bar

Scroll Bars

55

 **2** Click the Maximize button to view the window using the whole screen, and the Restore button appears in place of it

Application Windows

Application programs, even ones included in Windows 10, may still use the traditional window structure, with a Title bar and Menu bar. For example, the Notepad application window:

1 Select Start, All Apps, Accessories, then Notepad, then type some text (or open an existing file)

Control Icon   Title Bar   Menu Bar   Scroll Bars

Typing cursor

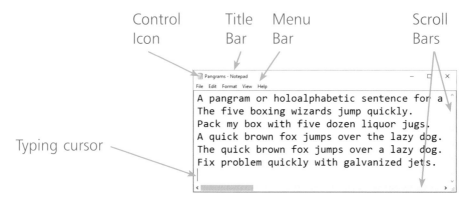

Other Windows 10 applications such as WordPad and Paint use the Scenic Ribbon in place of the Menu Bar.

1 Select Start, All Programs, Accessories and WordPad, and then open a file (or type some text)

File Tab   Quick Access Toolbar   Tabs   Ribbon

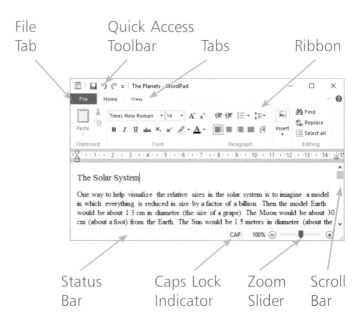

Status Bar   Caps Lock Indicator   Zoom Slider   Scroll Bar

Some applications may not use all the features, e.g. Character Map uses a window with no scroll bars, and cannot be resized.

Menus and Dialogs

The entries on the Command bars, Menu bars and Ribbons expand to provide a list of related options to choose. Some entries expand into a sub-menu, for example:

1 Open the Libraries folder, select Documents and click Manage, then click Set save location. Note the sub-menu for Set public save location

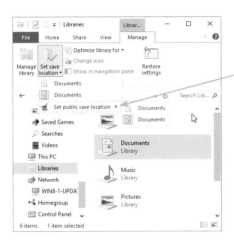

The black triangle next to a menu entry indicates that there are additional options available to be displayed.

Other commands open dialog boxes that allow you to apply more complex configurations and settings. For example:

1 In the Libraries folder, select the Home tab, and then click the Properties button

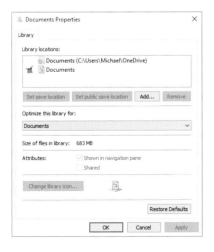

2 The Properties panel is displayed

3 Make changes and click OK to apply, or click Restore Defaults to undo

Some entries are toggles that switch on when selected, then switch off when reselected. For example, a ✓ symbol, may be added to or removed from a box.

Move and Resize Windows

Hot tip

Double-clicking on the Title bar has the same effect as the Maximize and Restore buttons.

Don't forget

To show a frame as you drag a window, in System Properties, select Advanced System Settings, Performance Settings and Adjust for best performance.

Hot tip

Dragging a corner of the window allows you to adjust the two adjacent borders at the same time.

1 To maximize the window, double-click the Title bar area (double-click again to restore the window to its original size)

2 To move the window, click the Title bar area, hold down the mouse button and drag the window

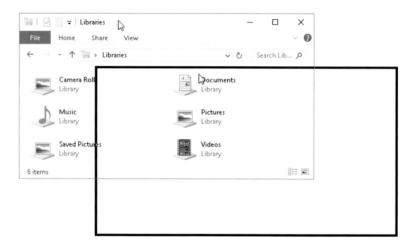

3 To resize the window, move the mouse pointer over any border or any corner

4 When the double-headed resize arrow appears, click and drag until the window is the desired size

Snap

On the Windows 10 Desktop, the Snap feature offers ways to move and resize windows in one step.

Maximize the Window

1 Drag the Title bar to the top of the screen

2 The window's outline expands to fill the whole Desktop

3 Release the Title bar to maximize the window

Expand Vertically

1 Drag the top border of the window to the top of the screen

2 The window's outline expands to the height of the Desktop

3 Release the Title bar to maximize the height but maintain the width of the window

Half or Quarter Screen

You can move the Classic app window to the side or corner.

1 Drag the Title bar to the left or right edge and release it there for a half screen

2 Drag the Title bar to any corner and release it there for a quarter screen

You can also drag the bottom border to the bottom edge, to expand the window vertically.

To return the dragged window to its previous size and position, just double-click on the Title bar.

Universal Windows Apps

When you are working in Desktop mode, the windows for your Universal apps operate just like those for Classic apps, with Cascade, Resize, Maximize, Minimize and Close, etc.

Hot tip

In Tablet mode, all app windows are full-screen. They can be minimized but cannot be resized, except via the Snap options (see page 40).

However, there is a minimum size for most apps. Weather and Money apps for example can be no less than 502 x 533 pixels.

Start Menu

The Start menu panel operates like a window, but with limitations. There's a vertical scroll bar, and you can drag the top and right edges, but the panel resizes in stages. The bottom-left corner is fixed in position, and there's no Title bar and no Minimize, Maximize or Close buttons.

Don't forget

You can make the Start menu full-screen via Settings. Open Personalization and select Start, then turn on the toggle for Use Start full screen.

This will look like Tablet mode, but you'll still have the Classic and Universal apps.

④ Personalize Your System

In this chapter you will learn how to change the appearance of the Windows 10 Lock screen and Start menu, add an account picture, organize the tiles and the apps, manage your user account, add a picture password or PIN code and take advantage of ease of use features. You can also personalize the Desktop environment and manage the display options, including screen resolution and multiple displays.

Settings

Windows 10 provides the Settings function to make changes to your system, and (if you use a Microsoft Account) you can apply those changes when you sign in to a different PC.

You can open Settings by clicking All Settings in the Action Center (see page 32).

There are several ways to open Settings:

1 Select Settings from the Most Used list on the Start menu

2 Select Settings from the alphabetic All Apps list

3 Press the WinKey + I to open Settings

4 Open File Explorer, select This PC, then Computer and click the Open Settings button on the Ribbon

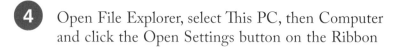

Press WinKey + X, or right-click the Start button, to display the Power User Menu (see page 36) and select the entry for the Control Panel.

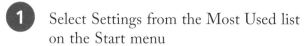

Windows 10 also includes the Control Panel; the application provided in all versions of Windows for changing settings.

Personalize Lock Screen

The Lock screen appears when you start Windows 10, sign out or resume from Sleep. To customize this screen:

1 Open Settings (see previous page), click Personalization and then select Lock screen

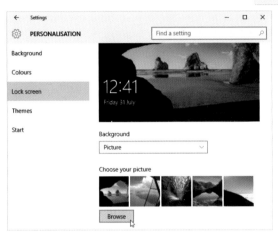

2 Scroll down and select one of the supplied pictures to make it the background image

3 Alternatively, click Browse to select an image from your Pictures library or from a different image folder

4 Scroll further down the Lock screen settings pane, to choose Apps which can display live notifications, updates, a quick status, or alarms

...cont'd

Hot tip

You don't have to save the changes or close the Settings function to apply the changes. The updates will be applied immediately.

5 Click the existing App icon or the Add icon and select the desired app that will display a detailed status or alarms (or select None to remove a selection)

6 Similarly, you can choose apps to show a quick status (or select None to remove a selection)

You can view your changes to the Lock screen immediately. To do this:

1 Switch to the Start menu and right-click the username or the user picture

2 Select Lock to display the Lock screen, whilst still retaining your session (but not Sign out, since that ends the session)

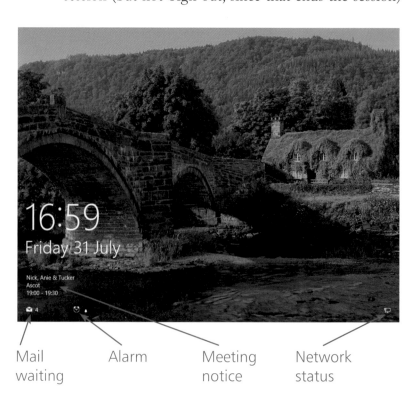

Mail waiting   Alarm   Meeting notice   Network status

Don't forget

You will have status indicators in the form of icons, e.g. Network for connected PCs and Power for battery PCs.

Desktop

1 Open Personalization and then select Background

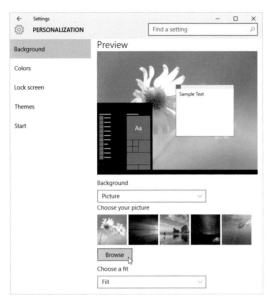

The background can be a picture, a slideshow or simply a solid color. The image may fill the screen, fit to height, stretch both ways, tile, center or span across multiple monitors.

2 Choose Picture from the drop-down menu and select an image to act as the background for the Desktop

3 You can also click Browse and select an image from your Pictures library or another image folder

4 Select Start, to control what items are on the left-hand side of the Start menu

5 Select Colors, to apply a color accent to the Taskbar, window borders and the Start menu

6 Select Themes, to apply predefined sets of colors, images and sound effects, and other related settings

Themes opens the Theme Settings option from the Appearance and Personalization section in the Control Panel (see page 79) as used in previous versions of Windows.

Select Start and click the Show more tiles toggle to arrange tiles in blocks of 4x4 rather than 3x3.

If you are signed in with a Microsoft Account, your choices will be applied to any Windows 10 PC you sign in to with that Microsoft Account.

Account Picture

You can specify a photo or image that will be used alongside your username on the Start menu:

1 Open Settings and select Accounts, or right-click the username on the Start menu screen and select Change account settings, then click Your account

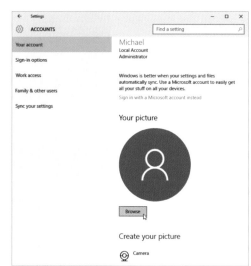

Don't forget

You can select or create a picture of any size and it will be converted to the appropriate size for use with the Start menu or other functions related to the Microsoft Account.

2 Click Browse to select an existing photo or other image from your Pictures library or another folder

3 Alternatively, if your computer has a webcam or built-in camera, select Camera to take a picture

4 You can take a still photo or a video, but the video is limited to five seconds

5 Press the Windows key to toggle between the Settings screen and Start menu, to see the results

Beware

You can change the user image from any Windows 10 PC, but to remove it completely, you may need to sign in to your Microsoft Account using a web browser and amend your profile there.

If you are signed in with a Microsoft Account, the selected image will be displayed on the Start menu of any Windows 10 computer that you sign in to.

Manage Tiles

The app tiles displayed on your Start menu will depend on the choices made by the manufacturer or supplier of your computer, and may be in no particular order or sequence, but you have full control and can resize, rearrange, remove and add tiles as it suits you.

Choose Tiles

The first task is to choose a tile. You can't just click or touch it, since that will run the associated program. Instead:

1 To choose a tile with the mouse, right-click the tile and the context menu appears

2 Select the required action, or click Resize to see the options

The actions offered depend on the particular app selected. For Money, you can Unpin from Start, Resize, Turn live tile off (or back on), Pin to taskbar (or unpin) and Uninstall.

You can choose from up to four sizes of tile – three square sizes (Large, Medium and Small) and one oblong size (Wide). For some Universal apps, the choice is more limited, and even more so for Classic applications, for example:

3 Select a Universal app such as Search and you'll see three tile sizes offered – Small, Medium and Wide

4 Select another Universal app such as Settings and you may see just Medium and Small sizes, as you do for any Classic app, e.g. Access

Hot tip

With a touchscreen, touch and hold the tile, to access buttons to Unpin and More options. Touch the latter to see all the actions offered.

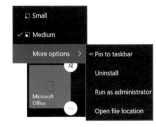

Don't forget

Select and hold a tile, and drag it into a new position and the tiles will automatically reflow. This will also happen when you Unpin or Resize tiles.

...cont'd

As always, the options offered vary depending on the type of entry selected and its current status.

Click the Expand arrow next to an entry, for example Windows Accessories, to show all the items it includes.

5 Right-click the Windows Store app to see the actions that are offered for this Universal app

You can Unpin from Start, Resize, Turn live tile off or Unpin from taskbar, but there's no option to Uninstall.

Add Tiles

The All Apps screen is the usual place to locate apps and add their tiles to the Start menu.

1 In Tablet mode, select the button to display Most Used/Recently Added

2 In either mode, select All Apps and scroll through the list to see all the entries

You'll see all the Universal and Classic apps that are installed on your system, listed alphabetically by name. Some apps are grouped, for example Windows Accessories, Ease of Access and System, plus Microsoft Office Tools (if installed).

Any other apps that you subsequently download and install will also be included in the list.

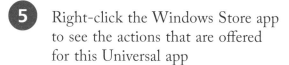

Manage Apps

Select Universal or Classic apps of different types to see what actions are offered:

1 Select a Universal app that's currently on the Start menu and you can Unpin from Start, Pin to taskbar or Uninstall

2 For a Universal app not currently on the Start menu, you can Pin to Start, Pin to taskbar or Uninstall

3 Select a Windows Accessory such as Paint and you can Pin to Start, Pin to taskbar, Run as administrator or Open file location

4 If the Windows Accessory or Classic app is already pinned to Start, you get Unpin from Start, Pin to taskbar, Uninstall, Run as administrator and Open file location

Don't forget

You can add items from the Desktop to the Start menu, such as disks, libraries and folders. Right-click the item in File Explorer and select Pin to Start from the menu.

69

5 You can right-click any entry in the Most Used or Recently Added sections of the Start menu, where you'll see the additional option: Don't show in this list

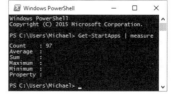

You can find out how many apps you have in your system.

1 Run Windows PowerShell and enter the command **Get-StartApps | measure** and the total number of apps is displayed

2 Type Exit to leave PowerShell

Hot tip

To run PowerShell, Select All Apps and find Windows PowerShell, or type Powershell on the Start menu and press Enter.

Create a Group

Only a few of the apps on your system are included as tiles on the Start menu, so you must add those you want. You can then arrange them in groups so they are easy to locate:

1 Select each accessory or Office app in turn, and choose Pin to Start

2 The apps you pin are added after the existing apps, with no automatic grouping

...cont'd

3 To create a group for the Accessories, select one of them and begin to drag it towards an empty space

4 When the bar appears, release the tile to drop it into the new group

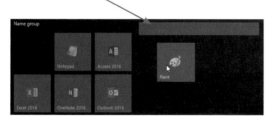

5 Drag and drop other Accessories into the new group

6 We now have two groups, one for Office and one for Accessories, though at this point neither is named

Name the Group

1 Point and hover or Touch above the group and the Name group option is displayed

2 Click Name group, and a typing area is presented

3 Type a name for the group, e.g. Windows Accessories, and click an empty part of the Start menu to apply the name

4 Repeat this procedure to add the name for the other group, i.e. Microsoft Office 2016

5 There are now Group name headers for both groups

Hot tip

You can reorder (and resize) the tiles in a group, for example by putting the most used apps at the top.

6 To change or delete a Group name, click in the Group name to reveal the typing area, make the change, and then press Enter

Change User Account

1 Open Settings, select Accounts, then Your account

2 If you are signed in with a Local Account, you can switch to a Microsoft Account instead

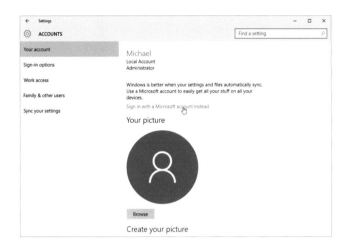

3 If you are signed in with a Microsoft Account, you can switch to a Local Account instead

4 In either case, you can change your password, create a picture password, create a PIN or add a new user

You'll be asked to provide an email address, which may be an existing Microsoft Account, or one that can be used to create such an account.

You must provide a username, password and password hint to aid signing in to this computer. Note that as a Local Account, it will not be synced with your other Windows computers.

PIN is an acronym for Personal Identification Number and here it is a four digit code (see page 76).

Picture Password

Don't forget

You'd normally use picture passwords with a touchscreen, but it is possible to use a mouse.

Don't forget

The picture password consists of three gestures, applied in sequence at specific locations. You can choose one or more types of gesture – draw a circle, draw a straight line or tap the screen at a point.

1 Open Settings, select Accounts, Sign-in options and then Add (underneath Picture password)

2 Type your password to verify the account, then click OK

3 Select Choose picture, find a suitable picture file, then click Open

4 Follow the prompts to position the picture, draw the three gestures and confirm your gestures

Hot tip

If needed, you can start over to enter a new set of gestures, if you are having trouble repeating your initial selection.

...cont'd

5 When you've successfully confirmed your gestures and your picture password is set up, click Finish

The next time the Lock screen appears and you sign in, you'll be able to use your picture password.

6 If you wish, you can select Sign-in options to switch to the normal password sign-in procedure

The selected gestures – a circle, a line and a tap – are shown here for example, but such indicators will not normally appear on the display, except when you are having problems during the initial setup.

You can use Windows Hello to sign in if your PC is set up for it. Go to Start, select Settings, Accounts and Sign-in options. Under Windows Hello, you'll see options for face, fingerprint or iris if your PC has a fingerprint reader or a camera that supports it. Once you're set up, you'll be able to use Windows Hello to sign in.

PIN Code

Don't forget

The PIN code consists of four digits and is mainly intended for tablet PCs, but can be set up on any type of computer running Windows 10.

Hot tip

You can return to Settings at any time to change your PIN code (or reset a forgotten PIN code).

76

Beware

PIN codes (and picture passwords) apply only to the specific computer on which they are set up and will not be transferred to other computers.

1 Open Settings, select Accounts, then Sign-in options, and then select Add (underneath PIN)

2 Enter your password to verify your account and click Sign in

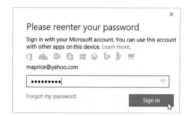

3 Enter four digits for the PIN and re-enter the numbers to confirm the PIN code

4 On a tablet PC, select the entry box for the PIN, to display the touch keypad for numeric entry

5 Select OK when the values have been entered

When you next sign in, you'll be asked for the PIN, which you can enter by keyboard or touch. Just provide the four digits – there's no need for the Enter key.

Click Sign-in options if you want to switch between the picture password, your Microsoft Account password, and the PIN code. All three are valid.

Ease of Access

Windows 10 Settings also allows you to set up Ease of Access options on your computer, to improve accessibility.

1 Open Settings, select Ease of Access and review the categories listed

2 Select Magnifier to turn Magnifier on, invert colors and enable tracking (to have Magnifier follow the keyboard focus or the mouse cursor)

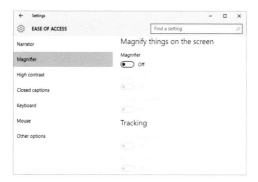

3 Select Mouse to adjust the pointer size, change the pointer color or use the numeric keypad to move the mouse around the screen

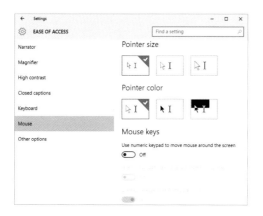

4 You can also manage use of the screen, keyboard and other options such as cursor thickness

You'll find help and guidance for using the options in the Ease of Access Center in the Control Panel (see page 82).

To make the typing cursor easier to spot, select Other Options then drag the slider for Cursor thickness until it is the size you'd like.

Select Narrator to turn on the screen reader for text and controls, choose a voice, select sounds and manage keyboard and mouse actions.

Open Control Panel

In previous versions of Windows, the most comprehensive options for customizing your system were provided via the Control Panel. Although the Settings feature is gradually taking over, the Control Panel is still important, so there are several ways to access this:

1 From the Start menu Search box, start typing Control Panel. When the Control Panel entry appears, press Enter or click it

2 From the Desktop, with Show desktop icons enabled (see page 52), double-click the Control Panel icon (if that icon is enabled for display)

3 Open File Explorer from the Taskbar, or the Start menu, select This PC and then the Computer tab, and choose System properties from the ribbon

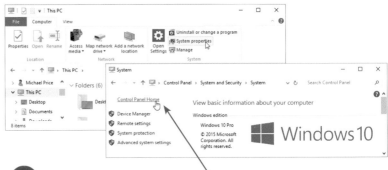

4 In System properties, select Control Panel Home

Hot tip

Select All Apps from the Start menu and scroll to Windows System, where you will find an entry for Control Panel.

Don't forget

You can also open the Control Panel from the Power User Menu (see page 36).

Personalize via Control Panel

Some options for personalizing the Desktop are still found in the Control Panel. To personalize your system:

1 Select the Appearance and Personalization option

Appearance and Personalization
Change the theme
Adjust screen resolution

2 Select Personalization to adjust the Desktop settings

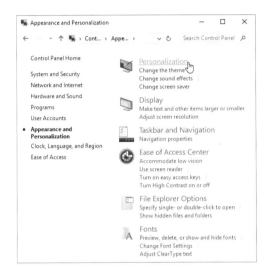

Control Panel options are still used to adjust settings for Themes, sound effects and screen savers.

3 Choose a theme or change individual characteristics

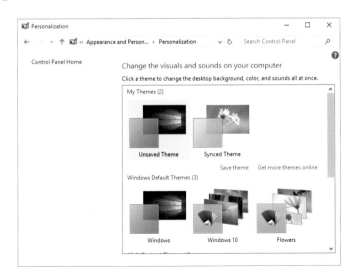

Other changes to the Desktop such as background and color must be made through the Settings app (see pages 62 and 65).

Display Settings

Don't forget

Display options other than resolution affect the Classic apps only and do not affect the Start menu and Universal apps.

Hot tip

You can also change the screen resolution via Settings. Right-click the Desktop and select Display settings (or open Settings and select System, Display) then select Advanced display settings.

1 From the Control Panel Personalization category, select the Display option

Display
Make text and other items larger or smaller
Adjust screen resolution

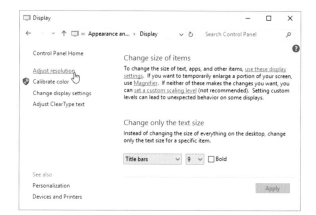

2 You can change the size of text and other items, or you can click Adjust resolution to change appearance settings

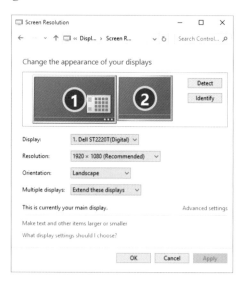

3 From here, you can set the resolution for your screen, choose the orientation and manage how multiple displays are used

...cont'd

4 Click the down arrow next to Resolution

5 Drag the slider to select a new resolution, then click OK

The higher the resolution, the more you can fit on the screen, but the smaller the text and images will then appear.

6 Click the down arrow next to Orientation to select Landscape or Portrait, or flipped if desired

7 If you have multiple displays, select how they will be used

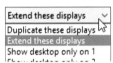

You can duplicate the screen contents, extend to use both (one being the main display) or just use a single screen.

8 After making the changes you want, select Apply

You will be asked to confirm that you want to keep the changes you have made.

9 After making the changes you want, click Keep changes

To cancel the changes, select Revert, or simply wait for 30 seconds and the changes will be automatically reversed.

Projector
You can also manage how a projector/screen will relate to the PC screen. As with multiple displays, you have the options of duplicating the contents, using the two screens separately or having just one of the screens active.

The screen thumbnails will change to reflect the resolution and orientation changes. You can also drag and drop the thumbnails to match the physical arrangement.

The resolutions, color settings and connections offered depend on the type of monitor and the type of graphics adapter that you have on your computer.

81

Ease of Access Center

Hot tip

If your PC has a microphone attached, you can use it for Speech Recognition, to dictate to the computer or to issue commands to control the computer.

Don't forget

The magnifier is not just for text, it is also very useful for close-up views of images of all types, including graphics, buttons and pictures.

Hot tip

Scroll down the settings and select Make the mouse easier to use, and you can turn on mouse keys and the numeric keypad to move the mouse around the screen.

1 From the Control Panel select the Ease of Access category

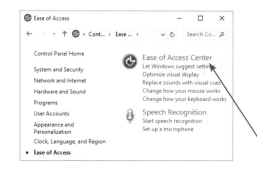

2 For an explanation of the options available, select the green Ease of Access Center link

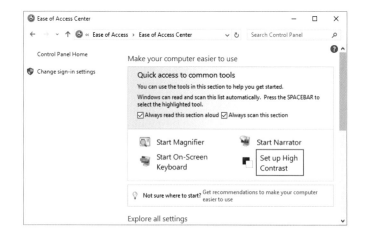

3 Start the main tools – Magnifier, Narrator, On-Screen Keyboard, High Contrast

4 If you are unsure, you can ask for recommendations to make your computer easier to use

5 Scroll down to explore settings, to optimize the computer for limited vision, set up alternatives for input devices and sound and make touch easier to use

5 Search and Organize

Windows 10 helps organize the files and folders on your hard disk. Data is stored by username with separate folders for different types of files, or you can add new folders. Libraries allow you to work with a group of folders. Powerful instant search facilities help you find your way around the folders and the menus.

Files and Folders

The hardware components are the building blocks for your computer, but it is the information on your hard disk that really makes your computer operate. There is a huge number of files and folders stored there. To get an idea of how many:

1 In the Desktop or Start menu Search box, type Computer and click This PC from the results

2 In the File Explorer window that appears, double-click the Local Disk (C:) to open it

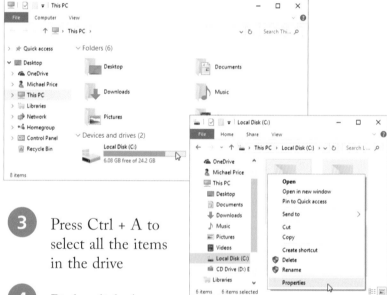

3 Press Ctrl + A to select all the items in the drive

4 Right-click the selection and click Properties

5 This example shows totals of almost 110,000 files and 22,000 folders on the C: drive

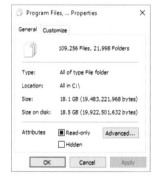

With so many files and folders to handle, they must be well organized to ensure that you can locate the documents, pictures and other data that you require with ease. Windows helps by grouping the files into related sections, for example:

- Program Files   Application programs (64-bit)

- Program Files (x86)   Application programs (32-bit)

- Program Data   Application data files (hidden)

- Windows   Operating system files & data

- Users   Documents, pictures, etc.

These are top-level folders on your hard disk and each one is divided into subfolders. For example, the Program Files folders are arranged by supplier and application.

1   Open the C: drive, then double-click Program Files, (x86) then Adobe and then the Reader subfolders

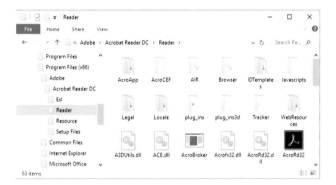

2   Move the mouse pointer over the Navigation pane and you'll see arrows next to some folders

3   The gray arrow symbol (❯) shows there are subfolders within that folder, and the black symbol (⌄) means it is at least partially expanded

Don't forget

On a 32-bit Windows system there is just the Program Files folder which then holds 32-bit programs such as Adobe Reader.

Hot tip

The Users folder contains Documents, Pictures, Music and other folders for each user defined on the computer.

Hot tip

The gray and black arrow symbols also appear when you select any of the folder names within the Navigation pane.

85

New User Account

You can add other users as part of your family group, giving them an account of their own, with libraries and standard folders.

If the new user does not already have a Microsoft Account, you can create one as part of the process of adding the user's account.

Adults added to your family group can manage the settings for the children in the group.

1 Open Settings (see page 62), select Accounts and then select Family & other users, then click the Add a family member button

2 Choose to Add an adult, and provide the email address for the person's Microsoft Account

3 Click Next and follow the prompts to invite that user to join your family group and set the account up on the system, ready for sign-in

4 Add a child to your family group

As with the adult, an invitation to join the group is sent as an email, and the child's account is made ready for sign-in.

5 You can also add someone else to the PC, although not as a member of your family group, so no invitation will be issued

You can allow a new user to sign in while you are still logged on to the computer:

6 From the Start menu, click the current user and select the new user

7 From the Sign-in screen that appears, type the password and press Enter

Windows creates the user libraries and folders (see pages 92-96), and installs any necessary apps. Progress messages are displayed.

Setup completes, and Windows restarts with the new user account active.

Hot tip

Any new users that you create are added to the Family & other users section of the Accounts settings.

Don't forget

If you sign out, switch user or shutdown/ restart, the new username can be selected from the Sign-in screen.

Finalize New Account

Respond to Invitation

1 Open the invitation email sent to the new user and click the Accept Invitation button

2 Click Sign in and join to confirm membership and view details of adult and child members

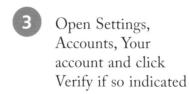

Verify Your Account

3 Open Settings, Accounts, Your account and click Verify if so indicated

4 Give your contact details, and enter the security code that you'll be sent via the selected method

Change Account Type

1 Open Control Panel and in the User Accounts category select Change account type

This displays details of all the accounts on your computer. You'll see that the first account, created when the system was originally set up, has been defined as Administrator.

2 Select one of the new accounts

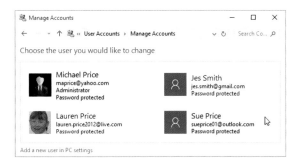

You cannot create new accounts from within the Control Panel. You must select the Add a new user in PC settings link, at the bottom of the Manage Accounts screen.

3 Select Change the account type and you'll see that it has been set as Standard

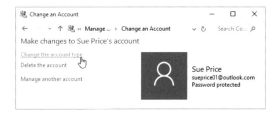

4 Select Cancel to exit without making any changes

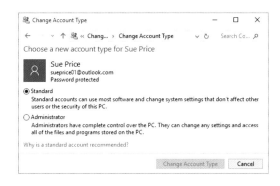

Standard user accounts are recommended for every user, even the Administrator. To minimize the risk of unintended changes, Windows will ask for the Administrator password when that level is needed.

Set Up Assigned Access

Don't forget

With Assigned Access you can restrict an account so that it only has access to one Universal app. This is for using the PC for a predefined function only, and is perhaps an alternative to the Guest user which appears to have been removed from Windows 10.

1 Open Settings and select Accounts, Family & other users and then Set up assigned access

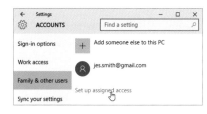

2 Click Choose an account and select one of the users from the list displayed

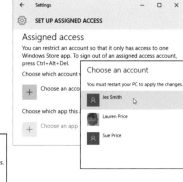

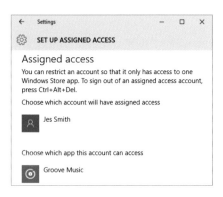

3 Click Choose an app and select the app that the user requires

4 Access to the specified app is now defined for the selected user

Don't forget

You must restart your PC to apply the changes and make the newly assigned account available for use.

5 To try out the new access, shut down and restart the system so that it displays the Lock screen

...cont'd

6 Select or swipe up on the Lock screen to display Sign-in

7 Select the user with Assigned Access and enter the password

8 The system starts up and the specified app is displayed, ready for use

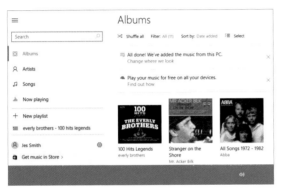

9 The Groove Music app, for example, will locate music on the system and make it ready to play

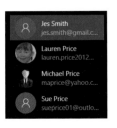

10 When the Assigned Access session is no longer required, you must enter Ctrl + Alt + Del to return to the Sign-in screen where you can shut down or switch users

Don't forget

Any data that the app needs must be preloaded, as it isn't possible to run any other apps while the Assigned Access app is running, since there's no Taskbar, no Start menu and no way to switch apps.

91

Beware

When you switch users from the user with Assigned Access and shut down, you may be told that there is still a user active, since you haven't explicitly signed out.

Someone else is still using this PC. If you shut down now, they could lose unsaved work.

Shut down anyway

User Folders

Documents and pictures that you create or save on your computer are kept in folders associated with your username.

92

1 Open the C: drive in File Explorer (see page 84) and double-click the Users folder

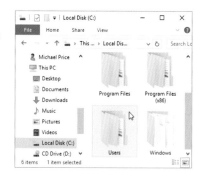

2 There's a subfolder for each user account name, plus the Public folder

3 Double-click the folder for the active user, in this case Michael

There is a set of subfolders with all the documents, pictures, data files and settings belonging to that user. There's also a link to OneDrive, the online storage for the user.

Each User folder (including the Public folder) has a similar set of subfolders defined.

The Documents, Music, Pictures and Videos folders can be accessed from This PC in File Explorer, and also from the Libraries link which can be added to the Navigation pane (see page 97).

This PC

This PC in File Explorer is a new feature in Windows 10. Like the Computer entry from previous versions of Windows, it provides a list of the storage devices and drives attached to the local computer.

1 Open File Explorer and click This PC

2 The lower group shows the Devices and drives, in this case the disk drive and the CD drive

In addition, however, File Explorer lists some of the folders associated with the active user.

3 The upper group shows folders for the current user, including Documents, Music, Pictures and Videos (the same folders as used by Libraries)

4 The Downloads and the Desktop folders are also listed in this group of folders

This PC replaces the Computer entry that you find in previous versions of Windows.

It also replaces (to an extent) the Libraries entry, though this can be reinstated (see page 96).

These are shortcuts, effectively linking to the actual folders on the hard disk of the PC.

OneDrive

OneDrive is Microsoft's cloud storage that comes with your Microsoft Account. You can have up to 5GB storage free, and access it from any device where you sign in with your Microsoft Account, or from any web browser. File Explorer gives local copies of folders kept in sync with your OneDrive:

1 Open File Explorer and select OneDrive in the Navigation pane to see the OneDrive folders that are kept locally, e.g. Documents, Music, Pictures

2 You can also click the OneDrive icon in the Notification area to Open your OneDrive folder

3 To select the files to sync, right-click the OneDrive icon and select Settings, then Choose folders

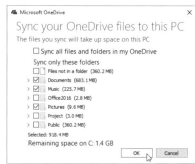

There may be other folders on your OneDrive that are not shown on your local copy. If you choose another folder, it will be added and its contents copied. If you deselect a folder, it and all its files are removed from the local copy.

Don't forget

The original feature was called SkyDrive but was renamed OneDrive for copyright reasons.

Don't forget

In previous versions of Windows, you needed a Classic app to access OneDrive. In Windows 10 you can use File Explorer to transfer files to and from OneDrive.

Hot tip

Only the folders you choose to sync will be shown in the local copy of OneDrive. Any changes you make are applied to the online OneDrive immediately, or the next time you connect to the internet.

4 Right-click the OneDrive icon and select Manage storage to see how much storage you have

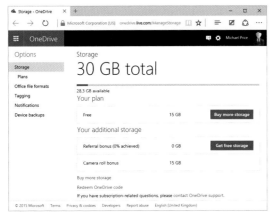

5 Microsoft gives you options to earn extra storage, or you can purchase additional blocks

If you are signed in with a Local Account, you may find OneDrive shown in File Explorer, but it will have no contents.

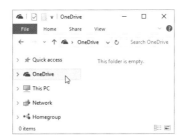

6 Select OneDrive from the Navigation pane and you are invited to set up OneDrive. You'll need a Microsoft Account to complete the procedure.

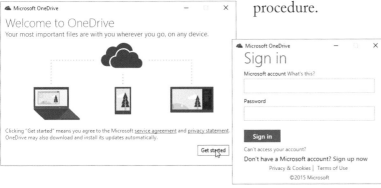

Hot tip

By default, you get 5GB of free OneDrive storage space with Windows 10 (the free allowance was reduced from 15GB in January 2016). This is an excellent way to back up your important documents, since they are stored away from your computer. For up-to-date information on plan allowances and pricing visit **https://onedrive.live.com/about/plans/**

Beware

If you sign in with a Local Account, the OneDrive entry may appear in File Explorer, but you cannot access OneDrive folders unless you provide a Microsoft Account.

Libraries

Libraries contain shortcuts to individual folders but allow you to treat the contents as if they were all in one folder. Typically, the Documents library would be a combination of the user's Documents folder and the Public Documents folder. This allows you to share documents with others (or access their documents). In Windows 10, Libraries are not displayed by default, but you can add them to File Explorer.

Don't forget

You can right-click any folder on your hard disk or OneDrive, select Include in library, and add it to any of your libraries, or use it to create a new library.

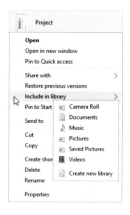

1 Open File Explorer, right-click the Navigation Pane and select the option to Show libraries

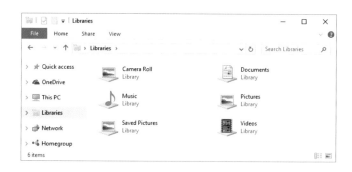

2 Select the Libraries entry that gets added, and you'll see the expected four libraries – Documents, Pictures, Music and Videos plus, perhaps, Saved Pictures and Camera Roll, used by the Photos and Camera apps

3 Double-click the Documents library and you'll see it has files from two locations – the user's OneDrive Documents folder (local copy of online folder) and the user's local Documents folder

Hot tip

By default, your OneDrive is set up for sharing documents, though you can revert to the local Public folders if you wish to share files on your local area network only.

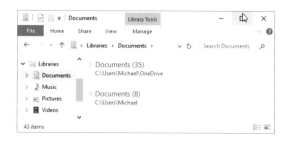

Folder Navigation

When you open a drive or folder, you'll find a number of different ways to navigate around the folders on your disk.

1 Open, for example, a subfolder in Pictures using File Explorer

Quick Access Toolbar   Tab Bar   Title Bar   Search Box   Help

Forward, Back

Up One Level

Address Bar

Navigation Pane

Contents Pane

Details Pane

Status Bar

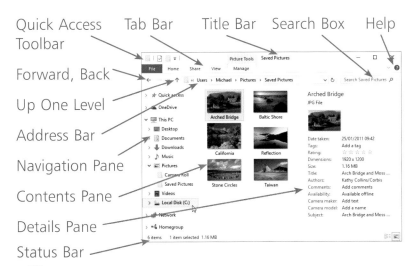

Click the Forward and Back arrows to navigate through locations you have already visited.

2 To go directly to a location on the Address bar, just click that location, for example the User's folder (in this case Michael)

The Address bar displays the current location as a series of links, separated by arrows. There's an Up arrow at the left, to go up one level.

3 To go to a subfolder of a location on the Address bar, click the arrow to the right of that location, and select a subfolder from the list displayed

4 To type a location, click the blank space to the right of the current location

5 The current folder address is highlighted

For common locations, you can type just the name, for example:
- Computer
- Contacts
- Control Panel
- Documents
- Pictures

6 Edit the folder address to the required location, for example C:\Users\Public\Pictures, and then press Enter to go to that location

Create Folders and Files

Hot tip

Create new folders to organize your documents by use or purpose, or create files of particular types, ready for use.

Don't forget

Choose one of the file types, for example a Microsoft PowerPoint Presentation, and it will be initially named as New Microsoft PowerPoint Presentation. Overtype this name, as shown for the New Folder in Step 3.

1 Open the library or folder where the new folder is required, for example select This PC, Documents

2 Right-click an empty part of the folder area and select New > Folder (or choose a particular file type)

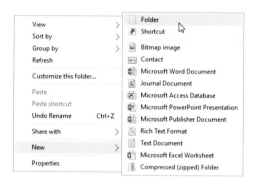

3 Overtype the name New folder with the required name and press Enter (or click elsewhere)

If you create a folder or a file in a library, such as Documents or Pictures, it will be created and stored within the library's default save location, for example the current user's My Documents or My Pictures.

Copy or Move Files

You can copy a file (or files) using the Windows clipboard:

1 Open the folder containing the file, right-click the file icon and select Copy (or press Ctrl + C)

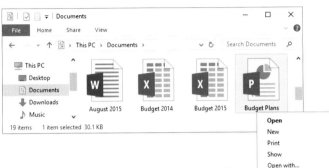

2 To copy multiple files, use the Shift or Ctrl keyboard keys to select multiple files before clicking Copy

3 Locate and open the destination folder, right-click an empty space and select Paste (or press Ctrl + V) to create a copy of the file in that folder

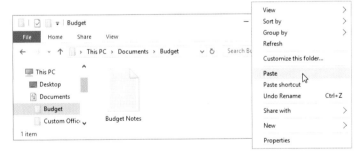

4 To move a file to a new location rather than make a copy, right-click the file icon and choose Cut (or press Ctrl + X)

5 The original file icon will be grayed out until you select Paste, when it will be moved to the new location

If your computer has a CD or DVD Writer, Windows 10 allows you to write files onto blank CDs or DVDs. E.g. to save files to disc as backups:

Insert your blank CD or DVD disc into the drive. From the Taskbar or Start menu select File Explorer. Your blank disc will appear under Devices and drives. Double-click it.

When the Burn a Disc box appears, type a name for your disc in the "Disc title" field and choose With a CD/DVD player, then click Next. Copy and Paste (or drag and drop) the files and folders into the disc window.

Right-click a clear part of the window and select Burn to Disc. Select the desired recording speed (slower gives better quality). Click Next. When the disc is ready, remove it and store it safely.

...cont'd

To move or copy files using drag-and-drop operations:

1 Use File Explorer to locate and open the folder containing the files you want to move

If the target folder isn't visible, locate it using the Navigation pane, clicking the gray arrows to expand the folders.

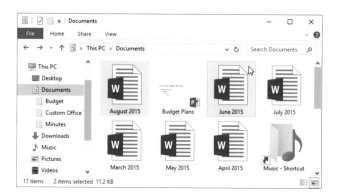

Drag using the Right mouse button rather than the Left. When you release the files, you get a menu to confirm the desired action (or Cancel).

2 Select the first file then press the Ctrl key as you select the second and subsequent files

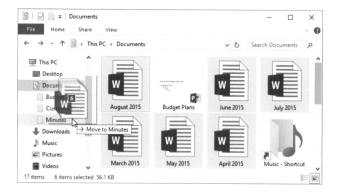

When the source and target folders are on different drives, the Shift key activates Copy, and the Ctrl key activates Move.

3 Click and hold any of the selected files, then drag the selection to the target folder and release there

4 To copy rather than move the files, `+ Copy to Minutes` hold down Ctrl as you drag and release the selection

5 If the target folder is in a different drive, hold down Shift as you drag to move, otherwise you will copy

Delete Files

To remove files from a folder:

1 Select the file or files, and either right-click the selection and choose the Delete command, or press the keyboard Delete key

2 If the file is located anywhere other than your hard disk, you are asked to confirm permanent deletion

3 Files on the hard disk are moved to the Recycle bin, usually with the warning message turned off

To recover a file deleted by mistake:

1 Right-click the Recycle bin and select Open (or just double-click the icon)

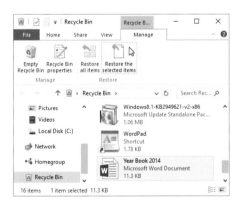

2 Select the file or files to be recovered and click Restore the selected items, on the ribbon

3 The files are returned to their original locations

To turn on the warning message for hard disk files, right-click the Recycle Bin, then select Properties and tick Display delete confirmation dialog.

To remove hard disk files completely without using the Recycle bin as an interim store, hold down Shift as you select Delete. You'll be asked to confirm. The deleted files then cannot be recovered.

You can also change folder views using the File Explorer Ribbon (see page 104).

Folder Views

File Explorer offers a variety of ways to view the files and subfolders contained in folders and libraries:

1 Open a library or folder, for example Saved Pictures, and note the file list style in use (i.e. Large Icons)

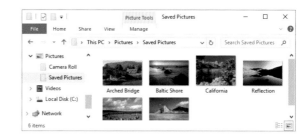

2 Right-click an empty part of the folder area and select View, to see the various styles, and the current setting marked with a bullet

3 Choose any of the four icon sizes to see the effects

The folders illustrated here have their layouts changed to hide the Navigation and Details panes (see page 105).

Extra Large icons   **Large icons**

Medium icons   **Small icons**

For icon sizes other than Small, you can select Hide file names from the View menu.

Other views can offer more information about the files.

List

Details

A file-type icon rather than a thumbnail is used for Small icons, List and Details views.

Tiles

Content

The details provided with the Content view depend on the file type, and on the data provided when the file was created.

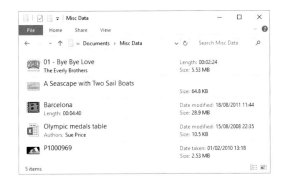

As with Views, you can also change Sort and Group attributes using the File Explorer Ribbon (see page 104).

The options in the Sort by and Group by menus also depend on the type of file that the folder has been optimized for i.e.

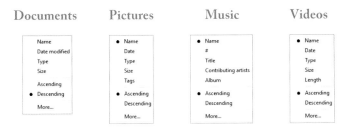

Documents

Name
Date modified
Type
Size
Ascending
● Descending
More...

Pictures

● Name
Date
Type
Size
Tags
● Ascending
Descending
More...

Music

● Name
#
Title
Contributing artists
Album
● Ascending
Descending
More...

Videos

● Name
Date
Type
Size
Length
● Ascending
Descending
More...

Don't forget

Where space permits, commands have icons with names. On narrower windows some become icons only, or get minimized to drop-down boxes.

File Explorer Ribbon

You can also manage the appearance of libraries and folders using tabs and command groups on the File Explorer Ribbon.

1 Open File Explorer and, for example, select the Pictures library

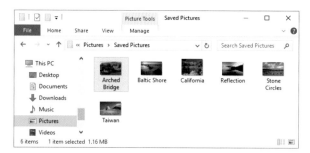

2 If there's no Ribbon, click a tab, e.g. the Home tab

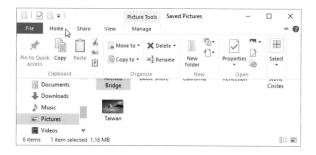

3 To always show the Ribbon, right-click the tab bar and click Minimize the Ribbon, to untick the option

The Ribbon shows commands appropriate to the specific tab and grouped by function. Inactive commands are grayed out.

The Home Tab
The Home tab has commands for handling items in the folder.

...cont'd

The Share Tab
These commands are to help you make files and folders available to other users.

The View Tab
With these commands you can control the layout of folders and the appearance of items in the folders.

The Manage Tabs
These are commands that are specific to the type of folder – Picture Tools and Library Tools as shown.

The File Menu
Select File to open new windows, access Help and Close File Explorer.

You can send files via email, write files to CD or DVD and set up sharing across the network.

The Current view category includes Sort by and Group by and Show/hide allows you to reveal hidden files.

The Manage tools displayed are based on the type of file for which the library or folder has been optimized.

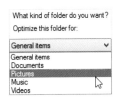

File Explorer Layout

You can control how libraries, folders and files are displayed in the File Explorer window. To illustrate the options:

1 Open File Explorer and, for example, select the Pictures library

In this example, File Explorer shows the Ribbon, Navigation pane and Contents pane (with Large icons).

2 Click Preview pane and choose the Details view, to choose the style of the Preview pane

In the Preview pane, you can see a preview or extended details of the selected file – useful when you use list views rather than graphical icons for the folder contents.

3 Click Details pane and select List view, to choose the style of the Details pane

Preview pane and Details pane act as toggles – select one to switch off the other, or reselect the active pane to turn both off.

...cont'd

4 Click the Navigation pane button to display or hide Show all folders, Libraries or the Navigation pane itself

Quick access has links to frequently accessed folders and recently opened files.

5 You can have the Navigation pane expand automatically to the currently-open folder

6 Show all folders puts the system folders, drives, libraries and network items in a hierarchical list starting at Desktop

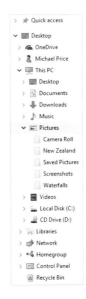

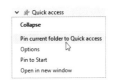

When you are in a folder you access regularly, right-click Quick access and select Pin current folder to Quick access.

7 To change the pane sizes, resize the window. Move the mouse pointer over the line separator and drag with the resize arrow to change the ratios of each pane

The preview shown depends on the file type. In the Documents folder, Word, WordPad or Notepad files can show text contents in the Preview pane. For other file types, you may see the message No preview available.

The preview image is automatically resized to make full use of the Preview pane, while retaining the image proportions.

To display just the folder contents in the File Explorer windows (as shown in the image on page 100), untick all of the Navigation pane options and deselect the Preview and Details panes.

107

Search Box

If you want to access a file, but are not sure which subfolder it is in, you can start at the higher-level folder and use the Search box to find the exact location.

Hot tip

The Search looks for matches with file names, file types, text content, file tags and other file properties.

Hot tip

You don't have to worry about using capital letters. Use quotation marks to match to a phrase rather than individual words.

Hot tip

You can also find files and folders using Cortana, the Personal Digital Assistant.

Don't forget

At any stage, you can select the required file from the list of results and double-click to open or run it.

1 Open, for example, the Music library in File Explorer

2 Click the Search box and start typing the search words, e.g. love is all around

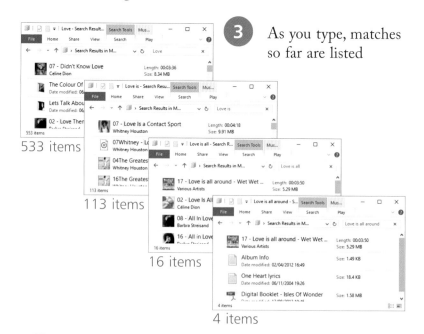

3 As you type, matches so far are listed

4 Stop typing when the results show the file you are seeking or when you have completed your search request

In the example, the results include a song of that title, related album information and the song lyrics.

6 Classic Applications

Windows 10 includes some useful Classic applications for calculating, text editing, word processing and picture editing and you can search the internet for external programs to handle other functions.

Classic Applications

Windows 10 provides the operating environment for a variety of applications. In many cases, these are supplied as separate programs or a suite of programs. However, some of the desired functions may be in the form of small but potentially very useful programs included with Windows under Windows Accessories. The main application areas and the included Windows programs are:

These applications take advantage of Windows 10 features and can be pinned as tiles on the Start menu, but they do not operate as Windows apps (see page 38).

● Text processing	Sticky Notes, Notepad
● Word processing	WordPad
● Electronic mail	Windows Fax and Scan
● Drawing	Paint
● Spreadsheet	Math Input Panel
● Database	Character Map, Steps Recorder
● Multimedia	Snipping Tool, XPS Viewer

You'll find these listed in All Apps, on the Start menu.

In addition, Windows 10 offers a variety of system and administrative tools.

You may have other Windows Desktop programs included as part of your system, such as Windows Media Player.

110

Some programs that were previously supplied as Windows Accessories are being provided as Universal apps e.g. Calculator, and Microsoft Edge (taking the place of Internet Explorer).

For functions that are not provided by the programs included with Windows, you'll need to install separate programs or a suite of programs such as Adobe Acrobat or Microsoft Office. If you don't want to install the full applications, you can download free readers and viewers, to display the files and documents that those applications create.

Notepad

Notepad is a text editor that you can use to create, view or modify text (.txt) files. It provides only very basic formatting, and handles text, a line at a time.

1 Search for Notepad in the Taskbar Search box, or select it from All Apps, open the program, then type some text, pressing Enter for each new line

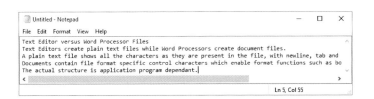

2 Select File, Save As and type the required file name (with file type .txt) then click Save

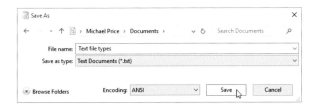

3 If the text is longer than the window, select Format and click Word Wrap, to fit the text lines within the window size

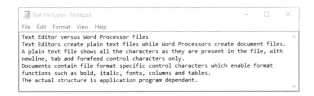

4 When you print the file, it will wrap according to the paper width, regardless of the word-wrap setting

The absence of formatting turns into a benefit when you are working with the source files for a program or the HTML code for a web page, since these require pure text.

Click Edit, Go To and then type a line number to go to a specific line in the file (as shown in the Status bar).

111

Go To is disabled and the Status bar is hidden when you select Word Wrap.

WordPad

WordPad also offers text editing, but adds tools and facilities for more complex formatting of individual pieces of text.

WordPad uses the Ribbon rather than a Menu bar. There are two tabs: Home and View. The File button provides Save, Setup and Print functions.

1 Start WordPad from All Apps, and enter text, pressing Enter for each new paragraph

Click the left, center or right alignment button to adjust the positioning of the selected paragraph or line of text.

2 Use the formatting bar to change the font, size, style and color for selected (highlighted) text

Save WordPad documents as .rtf (Rich Text Format) to retain the text formatting. Saving as .txt will remove the formatting (and images or links).

3 Click the Save button on the Quick Access toolbar (or press Ctrl + S) to save the document

Insert Pictures

WordPad also allows you to include pictures in documents.

1 Position the typing cursor and click the Insert, then the Picture button on the Home tab

2 Locate and select the picture, then click Open

Hot tip

You can also click the Paint drawing button, to insert a drawing that you create using Paint (see page 114).

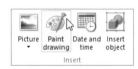

3 A copy of the image is added to the document and displayed at the cursor location

Don't forget

WordPad can open text files in a variety of formats, including Open XML, Unicode Text and Microsoft Office .docx (but not the older .doc format).

Rich Text Format (*.rtf)
Office Open XML Document (*.docx)
OpenDocument Text (*.odt)
Text Documents (*.txt)
Text Documents - MS-DOS Format (*.txt)
Unicode Text Documents (*.txt)
All Wordpad Documents (*.rtf, *.docx, *.odt, *.txt)
All Documents (*.*)

4 If it's the wrong size, right-click the picture, select Resize picture and choose the scale factor required

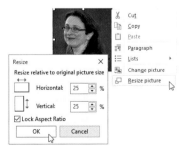

Paint

Paint is a digital sketchpad that can be used to draw, color and edit pictures. These can be images that you create from scratch, or you can modify existing pictures, such as digital photographs or web page graphics. For example:

1 Select Paint from the Start menu or All Apps, to start up with a blank canvas

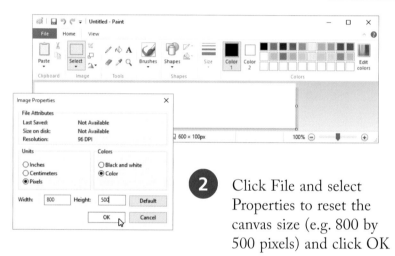

2 Click File and select Properties to reset the canvas size (e.g. 800 by 500 pixels) and click OK

3 Select the arrow below Paste, select Paste From, locate the picture to add to the canvas and click Open

4 Drag the image to position it centrally, with space for a title

5 Click Shapes, select the Rounded Rectangle tool, then click and drag to draw a frame around the picture

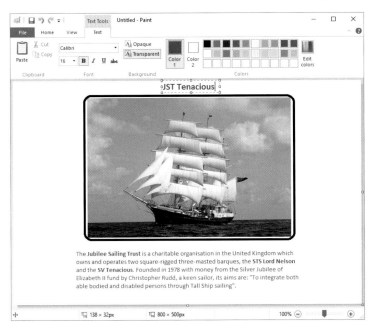

For a more realistic effect, draw a second frame outside the first and use the Fill tool to color the space between the frames.

6 Use the Text tool to draw a text box and add information such as a description of the contents

7 To make changes, select the View tab and Click the Zoom in button, or the Magnifier

8 When you've finished making changes, select File, Save, type the file name and click Save

Choose a suitable file type such as .jpeg for pictures, or .png for documents. Paint also supports .bmp, .gif and .tif file formats.

Unknown File Types

Windows and its applications cannot help when you receive attachments or download files of unknown file types, but will do its best to search for alternative options.

1 If there are unknown file types in your current folder, the extensions (normally hidden) are displayed

You can also right-click the file and select Open with, to get the initial suggestions.

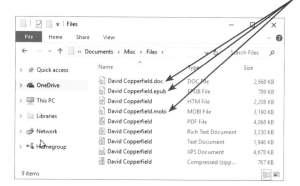

2 Double-click an unknown type, e.g. the DOC file, and you're asked how you want to open it

Beware

If there's nothing appropriate, just press the Esc key. Anything you do choose gets remembered, if you select the Always use this app... box, even if it doesn't work for that file type.

3 Click More apps to view the suggested programs. If none are suitable, select Look for an app in the (Windows) Store and click OK

Hot tip

If the Store does not find a good answer, you can search the internet for software, as shown on the following page.

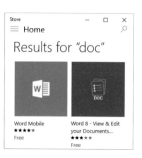

4 In this case, there are 92 apps in the Store that can work with DOC files, and of these, 63 can be installed free of charge

116

Search the Web for Software

If there's no obvious choice from the Windows suggestions, you can search the internet for suitable software.

1 To get information about the use and purpose of an unknown file type, visit **FilExt** at **http://filext.com**

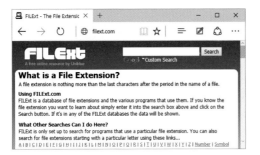

FilExt is a free online service by UniBlue, the PC Tools supplier. They, of course, take the opportunity to remind you about their products.

2 For a DOC file extension, select letter D from the index and scroll down to locate entries for .DOC

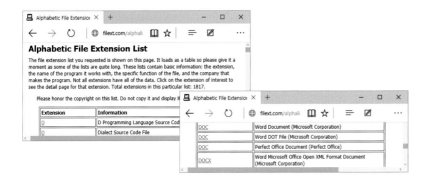

The .DOC extension has been used by many programs over the years. Microsoft Word is the most likely entry in this case.

3 Select the most appropriate entry, e.g. Word Document (Microsoft Corporation)

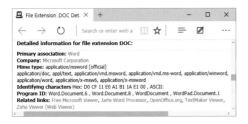

...cont'd

4 Open website **http://www.microsoft.com/download** and search for Word Viewer

5 Click the title link and follow the instructions to download the setup program and then run it

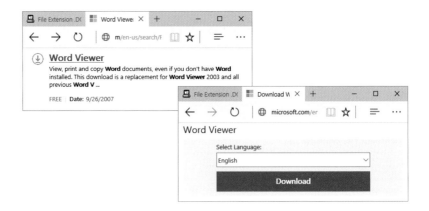

6 When prompted, accept the Terms and Conditions, and install Word Viewer onto your system

7 When installation completes, the .DOC files are recognized and will open in Word Viewer

Don't forget

An entry for Microsoft Office Word Viewer is added to the All Apps list (but by default it is not pinned to the Start menu).

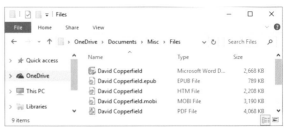

Change Default Program

With Word Viewer installed, you now have two programs which can load Rich Text Format documents. To review the options and confirm the default program for .rtf files:

1 Right-click any .rtf file and select Open with to list the programs available on your system

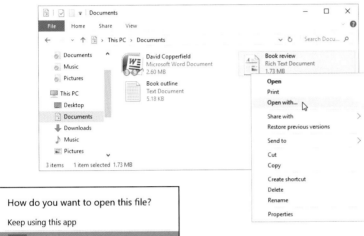

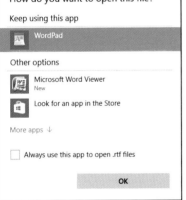

2 WordPad (the default) and Word Viewer are both shown

3 To change the default, select Word Viewer, click the Always use this app box, then click OK

4 The icons for the files indicate that the .rtf file uses WordPad as default, the .doc file uses Microsoft Word Viewer, while the .txt file uses Notepad

You can review and change the default program that is associated with any particular file type.

To open a file with a different program, without changing the default, choose the program and make sure the box is clear before clicking OK.

If you have Microsoft Office installed, it can open all three file types and may set itself as the default.

Hot tip

You can switch most PCs to Tablet mode, except those with multiple displays. You do not require a touch enabled monitor.

Don't forget

The Character map accessory is an exception in that it runs at its own fixed size in Tablet mode. This window can be moved, but again, cannot be resized.

Tablet Mode

The examples shown previously have all featured Windows apps running in the Desktop mode. These programs will also operate when the PC is in Tablet mode, but each program runs full-screen.

1 Start WordPad and Paint, and switch between them with Alt + Tab, or using the Task View button

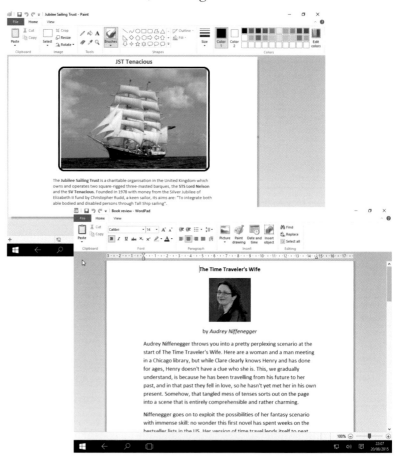

There are Titlebars, with Minimize, Maximize/Restore and Close buttons, but the Maximize/Restore buttons do not function, and the windows cannot be resized.

The Snap function is supported, so the screen can be split to run two programs side by side, each using half of the screen. However, the four-app split, positioning apps in all four corners of the screen (see page 41) is not supported in Tablet mode (*correct at the time of printing*).

7 Universal Apps

The emphasis is now on Universal apps in Windows 10. Some, such as Reader and OneDrive, are supplied at installation. However, there are many Universal apps at the Windows Store, where you can search, review descriptions, then download and install apps on your system.

Sources for Apps

Although Windows Classic applications are supported (see page 44), the main functions are provided by Universal apps in Windows 10. As already discussed, these can run full-screen or windowed, and can use Windows Snap to allow two or more apps to share the screen.

In the past, Windows applications have been available from many sources, including supplier and enthusiast websites, as well as Microsoft. Sources for Windows apps are now much more limited.

The primary design point for the Universal app is the touchscreen as exemplified by the tablet PC, but all the apps can also be operated on a system with standard monitor, mouse and keyboard equipment.

The Windows apps that are available can be found in just two places:

 Supplied and installed with Windows 10

This is a typical Start menu for a newly-installed Windows 10 system, showing some of the Windows apps you may expect to find installed.

All Universal apps must be submitted to Microsoft for certification before they are allowed in the Windows Store (or included on installation discs).

 Via Download and Install from the Windows Store

The range of Universal apps available at the Windows Store is expected to change frequently, as new products are added and others are removed or revised.

Programs submitted to Microsoft can also include Classic apps. These are conventional applications that are listed at the Windows Store, but provided from the manufacturer's website, via a link that is included with the application description. These and other conventional apps may still be obtained directly, without visiting the Windows Store.

Supplied with Windows 10

The details may change with updates to Windows 10, or with customization by your computer supplier, but these are the Universal apps that were initially included on the installation disc, or added during initial setup.

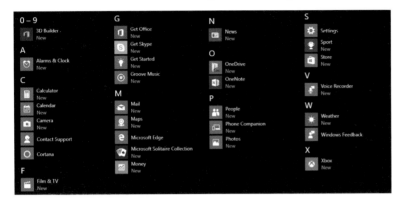

There are 29 Universal apps shown on this example of an All Apps list. Some of these apps feature on the Most Used or Recently Added lists. By default, 16 of them have Tiles on the Start menu. Those that are not shown can always be pinned to Start if desired.

There are four different sizes of tile, and you can select the size you prefer for each individual app. The Large and Wide options are particularly suitable for Live tiles that display real-time information. However, not all apps support the Large option and some apps are restricted to the Medium and Small options. To change the size:

1 Right-click the Tile and select Resize, and select from the options offered for that app

On the following pages we will look more closely at the Calculator, Alarm & Clock and other apps. Some of the apps, such as Mail, Microsoft Edge, Music and Photos, will be discussed in the relevant chapters on the specific topics.

Don't forget

To display the full list of apps, switch to the Start menu and click the All Apps button, at the bottom left.

In Tablet mode there's a similarly positioned button, but without the All Apps label.

Hot tip

You can also pin Windows accessories and other conventional Windows apps as tiles on the Start menu.

Calculator

While it is no substitute for a full spreadsheet application, the Windows Calculator app provides quite powerful computational facilities.

1 Select Calculator from the All Apps list on the Start menu

2 In Standard mode, type or click to enter the calculation using the desired operation symbol, and press = to display the result

Click the function buttons or press the equivalent keyboard keys, to perform Add, Subtract, Multiply, Divide, Square Root, Percentage and Inverse operations. You can also store and recall numbers from memory, and the History capability keeps track of stages in the calculations.

In addition to the Standard mode, there are also Scientific and Programmer modes, plus a variety of Converter options provided:

1 Open Calculator, then click the Menu button to list the modes

2 Select Scientific to see the features

Scientific mode offers a variety of logarithmic, trigonometric and factorial functions, in various forms, such as Degrees, Radians, etc.

...cont'd

3 Select Programmer mode just to see what it offers

The Programmer calculator operates in decimal, hexadecimal, octal and binary. It supports byte, word, dword and qword. There's a full keypad, including alphabetics for hex numbers, and an alternative bit-toggling keypad.

Unlike the other Calculator modes, Programmer mode does not maintain a history of computations.

There are 12 different Converter options, each with a range of units.

4 Select the Converter mode, and select a category, for example Weight and Mass, and choose the From and To units e.g. Kilograms to Pounds

Note how the Converter suggests equivalents, using other units including (in this example) footballs.

Each of the categories offers a range of appropriate units, and they all suggest equivalents to your results, sometimes quite idiosyncratic in nature:

5 Switch to the Energy category to convert between Food calories and Kilojoules

6 Enter 2500 as the starting value

You are told that this is about equal to 9914 BTUs or 9.99 slices of cake!

Weight and Mass has a total of 14 units that you can convert between.

Alarm & Clock

This app is a combination of an Alarm Clock, World Clock, Timer and a Stopwatch. You can use it to set alarms and reminders, to check the time anywhere in the world, and to time activities.

1 Select Alarm & Clock from the All Apps list (or search for it via the Search box)

2 Select each of the four types of clock in turn to review the features that are offered

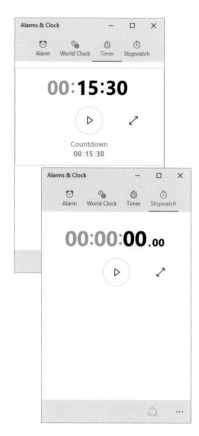

3 Click the New (+) button to add a new item, click the Manage button to remove items, and click More Options (...) to show additional commands

Weather

This app displays forecasts of temperature, wind direction and speed, humidity etc., for your default or chosen location.

1 Select the Weather tile from the Start menu to see the overview by day

2 Scroll down to see the details for the selected day

The Weather app runs on other devices such as tablets and smartphones, and adjusts itself to suit their particular screen sizes.

Select a specific day and view the Hourly Forecast, Summary or Details as desired.

Click the buttons on the Icon bar to display Maps, Historical Weather, Places or News. Click the Menu button to show categories for the button.

Windows Store

The Windows Store recognizes what version of Windows your system is running and displays apps appropriate for you. To see what's offered:

The Windows Store is the source for new Universal apps for your Windows 10 system, and is organized to help you identify useful items.

1 Touch or click the Store tile on the Start menu or the Store icon on the Taskbar to open the Home page for the Store

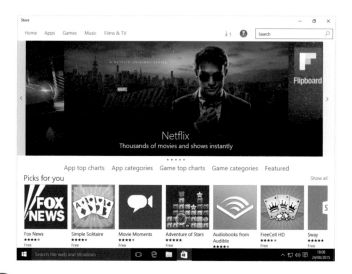

You can also scroll down the Home page to see sets of:

- Top free apps
- Top free games
- Top paid apps
- Top paid games
- Collections

Each displays a subset of apps, with a Show all link to see the full group.

2 You'll see highlighted apps scrolling horizontally, plus some Picks for you. Click Show all to see the full set of apps being suggested

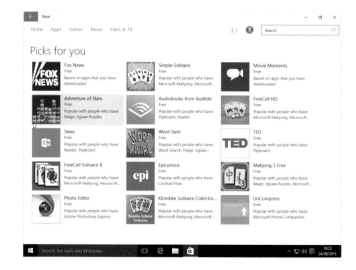

App Categories

To see what categories of apps are offered:

1 Select the Apps page and then select App categories

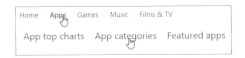

2 Scroll down through the list of categories, to review the 25 different groups provided

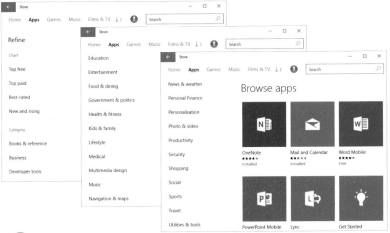

3 Click a group and browse apps, to view apps from that category

The entry for each individual app shows whether it is already Installed on your system, or available for download Free of charge, or requires payment (indicated by a price)

The price stated will be in the currency appropriate to your location e.g. Dollars for the USA, and Sterling for the UK.

Hot tip

The Windows Store for Windows 10 systems is arranged in various groupings, to help you explore its contents and find apps that are useful to you.

Don't forget

If one of the Chart options has been selected, for example New and rising, this will restrict the apps that are displayed. For a complete listing of apps, clear any refinement by clicking the X button.

Books & Reference

You can use the categories to explore the Windows Store's contents:

1 Select a category of interest, for example Books & reference

Category

Books & reference

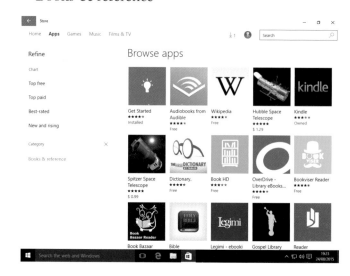

Don't forget

Each app in the Store is assigned to a specific category and subcategory. For Books & reference, the subcategories are:

E-reader
Fiction
Nonfiction
Reference

You can use the subcategories as search terms to help locate relevant apps.

2 Scroll down the screen to see more of the apps

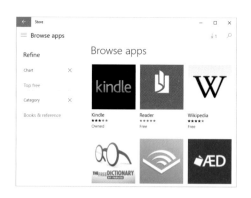

3 Select a Refine option such as Top free, to show only apps of that type in the selected category

Note that any apps you have installed on another system (using the same Microsoft Account), but not on the current system, will be shown as Owned. When you select such an app to view details, it will be shown as ready to install on the current machine.

kindle

You own this product and you can install it on this device.

Install

Search Windows Store

You can use the Search box found on every Windows Store screen to view its scope and find items of interest.

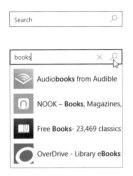

1 Select the Search box and type a search term, e.g. books

2 The top four matches are displayed immediately

3 Click the magnifying glass icon to show all of the results

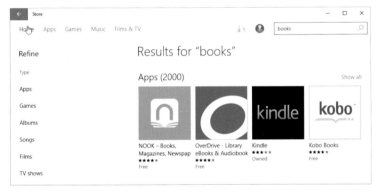

The app you want may not always be classified under the category you'd expect, so it is always useful to search the whole Store using your terms of interest.

You'll find varied results in multiple categories, such as Games, Albums, Songs, Films and TV shows, as well as in Apps.

4 Select the App group to refine the listing and show only the Available apps

Results for "books"
Apps (2000)
Games (20)
Albums (346)
Songs (2000)
Films (49)
TV shows (28)

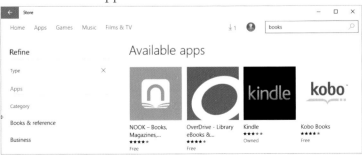

You can further refine the search results by selecting one of the 26 categories of app, or by adding an appropriate subcategory as a search term.

Installing Apps

Don't forget

If you already own this app, you'll see the Install button rather than the Free button.

Hot tip

During the process, messages from the Store let you know the progress of the actions being performed.

1 Find an app you want to investigate, for example Best Classic Novels

Best Classic Novels
★★★★★
Free

2 If you decide you want this app on your system click the Free button

 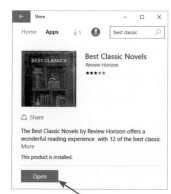

3 When the app downloads and installs, Open it directly from the Store entry

4 You'll also find entries for the app in Recently Added, and on the All Apps list

Right-click either entry in All Apps and select Pin to Start to add a tile to the Start menu.

Your App Account

From the Windows Store, you can check your account and see what apps you have installed, even if you use your Microsoft Account on multiple machines.

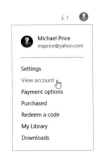

1 Open the Store app and click your User picture, then select View account from the User menu displayed

2 You will be asked to sign in with your Microsoft Account and password

Don't forget

Purchases include free apps as well as those you've paid for.

3 Your account is displayed with details of your recent purchases from the Windows Store

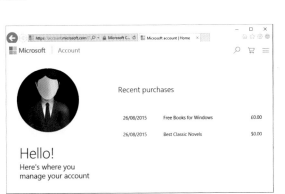

4 Scroll down to see details of all the devices associated with your Microsoft Account

Beware

You can install apps from the Store, free or charged, on up to ten Windows 10 devices, including PCs, tablets, smartphones and gaming devices, all associated with the same Microsoft Account, although you are limited to four Music and Video devices.

Your Library

1 From the Store app, click the User picture and select My Library

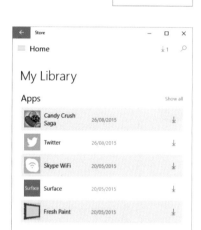

2 The recent apps you've downloaded and installed using your Microsoft Account will be listed

Don't forget

Click Show all to see all apps or games you have installed on any device using your Microsoft Account, as long as they are compatible with your current system (even if installed under an earlier Windows version).

3 Scroll down to see your recent games

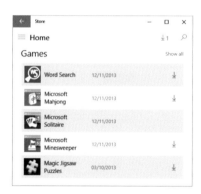

4 Select an entry to see its status on the current device

Hot tip

If you already own an app or game, but it's not installed on the current device, you'll see a Download button. This is not visible when the item is installed.

5 You can click the Download button to install an app or game on the current device

Updates

If any Universal app that you've installed gets updated, the changes are supplied through the Windows Store. In Windows 10, these updates are applied automatically in the background, without any notification.

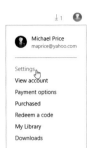

If you'd prefer to manually accept and install updates:

1 Select Settings from the User menu in the Store

2 Drag the button marked Update apps automatically to Off, to reverse the action and turn off updates

3 To view the Update status, select Downloads from the User menu in the Store

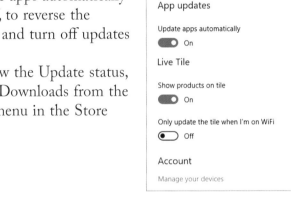

4 The available updates are listed and can be individually downloaded, or you can select Update all

5 Drag the button back to On again, to restore the automatic updating

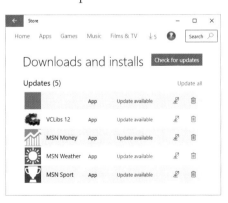

This option is not available on Windows 10 Home edition, so app updates will always be applied automatically.

When you drag a button on or off, it will change color from Blue (On) to Black (Off) or vice versa, to indicate the new status.

Verify Identity

For some actions within the Windows Store, you may be asked to verify your identity with a security code. For example:

Don't forget

You can select either an email address or a telephone number, depending what contact information is in the profile for your Microsoft Account.

1 Select Payment options from the User menu in the Store

2 If prompted, choose the method by which you would like to receive the security code

3 Complete the contact details and click Send code

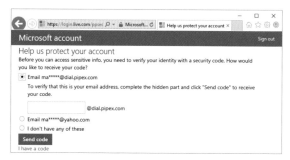

4 Enter the code that you receive and click Submit. Your account will then be verified by Microsoft and you will be able to use the Windows Store as normal

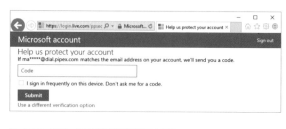

Hot tip

You may be prompted to use an app on your smartphone instead, so you can receive security codes at any time and any place, even if there's no phone service (see next page).

Authenticator App

1 From the screen on the previous page, select Set it up now for the Authenticator app

2 Choose the mobile device type, e.g. Windows Phone

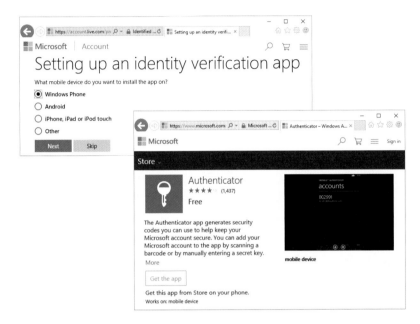

You can set up the Authenticator app on a Windows Phone, an Android device or an Apple iPad, iPod or iPhone.

3 Locate the Authenticator app from the Windows Store and install it on your device

Visit the Windows Store from your device and search for Authenticator, from the Microsoft Corporation. The blue and white key icon will help identify it.

4 Open the app and scan the barcode with your smartphone camera to pair the app with your Microsoft Account

...cont'd

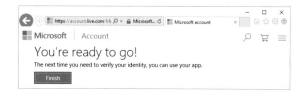

Hot tip

You can be added as a new user to any Windows 10 device, and use your Microsoft Account to sign in to that device.

The Authenticator app will be paired with your Microsoft Account and you can now use the app to verify identify:

1 When you sign in to a new device with your Microsoft Account, you need to verify your identity

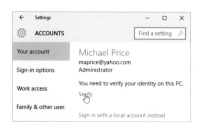

2 Click Verify and you are prompted for a code generated by your Authenticator app

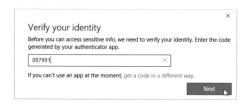

Don't forget

If your device containing the Authenticator app is not to hand, you can still use the email or phone methods for verifying your identity.

3 Open the Authenticator app on your mobile device, enter the code it displays on the new device, then select Next

4 Your identity will be confirmed, and you will have full capability on the device, including access to the Store

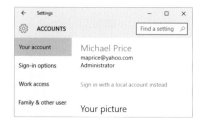

8 Email and Calendar

Windows 10 provides the Mail app for email communications, the People app to manage your contacts and the Calendar app to keep track of events and meetings. Communicate instantly using the Skype app. For email and time management you can also use Outlook from Office 2016.

Don't forget

An email address consists of a username or nickname, the @ sign and the server name of your email provider, e.g. jsmith99@myisp.com or web service e.g. jsmith99@gmail.com

Hot tip

The Skype app for messaging (and video and phone calls) is not installed, although there is a Get Skype link (see page 152) provided to make it easy to install when required.

Electronic Mail

Email or electronic mail is used to send and receive digital messages. You can send an email message to anyone with an email address, you can receive messages from anyone who knows your email address and you can reply to those messages, or forward them to another email address. You can send your email message to more than one person at the same time and attach files such as documents or pictures.

Email is free, since no stamp or fee is required. However, before you can use email, you require:

- An account with an Internet Service Provider (ISP)

- An internet connection such as telephone or cable

- A modem or router to make the connection

- An email address from your email service provider or from a web service such as Gmail or Hotmail

- An email program such as Mail or Outlook 2016

Mail
This is the Windows app that is installed along with Calendar and People, when Windows 10 is set up. It provides full-screen access to multiple email accounts.

Outlook 2016
This application is included in all editions of Microsoft Office 2016 except the Home & Student edition, and is installed with Windows 10 systems that have Office 2016 added. It provides fully functioning email and time management services, and runs on the Desktop as a windowed application (see page 155).

Other Email Programs
There are many other apps in the Windows Store which supplement the features of the Mail app. For example, Email Backgrounds provides colorful email stationery, while Email List Maker helps you extract and format email addresses from Word documents and spreadsheets.

Windows 10 Mail App

To get started with the Mail app:

1 On the Start menu select the tile for the Mail app

2 Click Get started

3 If you have just one email account that's the same as your Microsoft Account, you are Ready to go

Hot tip

Mail automatically detects your Microsoft Account and connects to that email service. This becomes the Outlook Account, even if your Microsoft Account is a non-Microsoft email.

4 If your email account is separate from your Microsoft Account, click Add account

5 Select your account type, for example Yahoo Mail, enter your email address and password, then click Sign-in

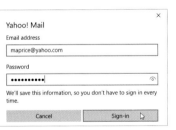

Don't forget

To add another email account, click Add account again, or click Ready to go if there are no more to add at this time.

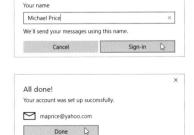

6 Specify your name as it should appear on your emails, then click Sign-in

7 Click Done when the account has been added successfully

...cont'd

When Mail starts up, the display you see depends on the screen resolution. On a higher resolution monitor, you'll see three panes – Accounts, Current Folder and Reading.

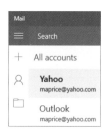

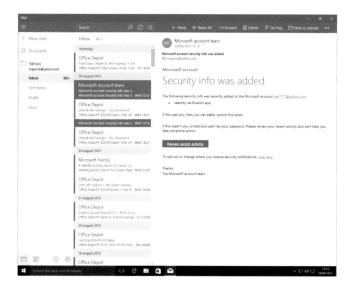

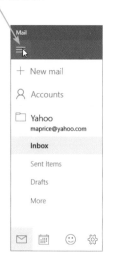
On a lower resolution monitor (the example below is 1024 x 768 rather than 1366 x 768 pixels) you'll see just the Current folder and Reading panes, plus a menu icon list.

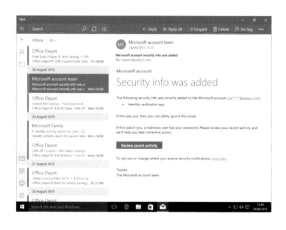

Mail App Settings

1 Click the Settings icon to show the options

2 Select Accounts to choose an account to edit its settings

3 Select Background picture to select an image for the Reading pane, displayed when no message is selected

4 Select Options to view or change Quick Actions, Email signatures and Notifications

5 If you have a Touch enabled system, you can carry out your most frequently used actions by swiping left or right. There are four possibilities to choose from for the two directions:

Set flag/Clear flag

Mark as read/unread

Delete

Move

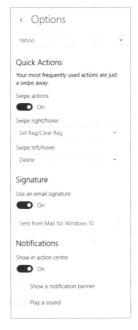

Don't forget

For a standard PC with keyboard and mouse, there are Quick Action Delete and Flag icons displayed when you move the mouse pointer over a message in the Inbox.

The Mail Window

These are the main elements of the Mail window:

- Accounts
- Mailbox Folder
- Reading Pane
- Respond
- Delete
- More Opti

- Selected Account
- Selected Folder
- Selected Message
- Folder List
- Feedback and Settings
- Mail and Calendar

Folder (Inbox) Contents   Message Contents

Hot tip

The Mail tile on the Start menu displays the message count and message extracts (even when the Mail app itself is closed).

---

1 Click the More Options button (...) at the top right of the window to display additional commands for dealing with the messages in your Mailbox

- Move
- < Previous
- > Next
- Print
- Q Zoom >

2 Click the Zoom button to list the scale factors offered

- < Zoom
- 400%
- 200%
- 150%
- 100%
- 75%
- 50%

3 Click the arrow to return to the Options, or click anywhere on the window to remove the list

View Messages

1 Select a message from the Folder contents and it displays in the Reading pane

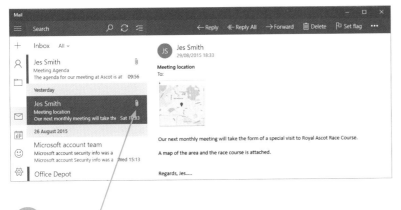

Pictures can be included in the body of email messages, as well as saved from them. Other files such as documents can also be sent, saved or opened from a message.

2 If there is an attachment (as indicated by a Paperclip icon) it will be contained within the email body or shown as a link

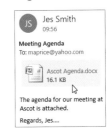

3 Click Reply to respond to the sender, Reply All to respond to all addressees, or Forward to send the message to another person

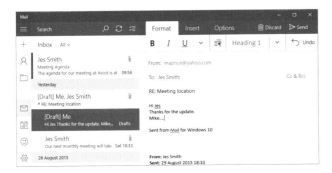

You can add recipients from your Contacts list (see page 148).

4 Type your reply and click the Send button when finished

5 A copy is saved in the Sent folder of the account used to send the reply

People

Windows 10 allows you to collect details of all your contacts and make them available to apps such as Mail and Calendar, via the People app.

Don't forget

The People app can manage all contacts associated with your email and personal networking, but you need to define which accounts to use.

1 Click the People entry on the All Apps list (or the tile on the Start menu if you've Pinned the app)

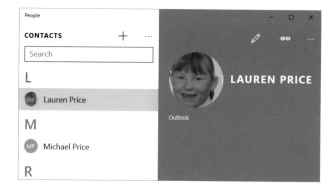

2 Click the More Options button (...) and select Settings to show the linked accounts

3 To start with, there may be just your Microsoft Account, with its associated contacts

Hot tip

The accounts that you add will be included in the list displayed by Settings.

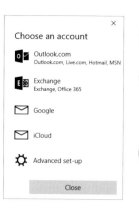

4 Click Add an account

5 Windows 10 will identify the types of account that have contacts that you may want to add

6 Follow the prompts to set up the account and add it to the Mail and the People apps

Managing Contacts

1 Select More Options then Settings, in the People app

2 Choose your preferred sort sequence, and how you'd like names to be displayed

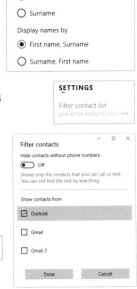

3 Select Filter contact list and you can choose to Hide contacts without phone numbers

4 You can also choose the accounts to show contacts from, to manage the size of the list

5 To work with a specific contact, click that entry

6 Select Edit to make changes to the details for the contact, selecting which account to change if needed

7 Select the Diskette icon to save the changes that you've made

Click the New button on the Contacts page and you can enter the details for a new contact.

Details for contacts include name, phone numbers, email IDs and addresses (home, work and other) plus notes. You can also add various extra fields:

Add a field
Website
Company
Job title
Office location
Significant other
Children
Birthday
Anniversary

Create a Message

You can select a contact in People and double-click the email address to open Mail, with a blank message addressed to that person.

How do you want to open this?

Keep using this app

Mail

Other options

Look for an app in the Store

Always use this app

OK

Don't forget

When entering contact names in the To: box, you may see several suggestions that match so far, but the number reduces as you enter more of the name.

1 In Mail, select the email account, go to the Inbox and click the New mail button (or press Ctrl + N)

+ New mail

2 A blank message is displayed, ready for recipient details and content

3 Begin typing the contact name in the To: box, then select the contact when it appears in the results below

4 Add more recipients in the same way, selecting from the suggestions where appropriate. Entries will be separated by semi-colons

5 Click in the Subject box and type the text for the title of the message

6 Click in the body of the message and add the salutation and the message text

7 End with your name, then the email signature for the sending account will be added automatically, if you have this set up (see Step 11 on the next page)

8 Select Cc & Bcc to add boxes for recipients who will be copied on the email

9 You can format the text in your message if you wish – click the Styles button to see more options

10 There are also Font formatting and Paragraph formatting options

11 To see your email signature, display the Mail Settings (see page 143), click Options and select the sending account

12 Click the Send button to send the message

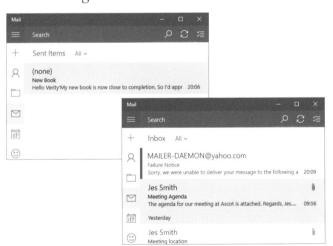

A copy of the message is kept in the Sent folder of the sending account.

Should there be any problems with the email addresses used for the recipients, you may receive a message from the Mail Delivery system describing the problem and its cause.

Hot tip

Recipients added using Bcc (Blind carbon-copy) will not be shown on the copies of the message that others receive.

Don't forget

Note that any changes to the signature text will not affect the current message but will apply to future messages only.

Don't forget

Sometimes a message to an email address may fail, perhaps because the domain server is offline for a period. After several attempts, an error response message may be returned to you.

Don't forget

You can switch between Mail and Calendar using the icons on the bottom left-hand panel or the Icon bar.

Hot tip

The first time you run Calendar, it lists the accounts (linked through Mail and People) and you can use their associated calendars.

Hot tip

You can choose which account calendar will be used to record the meeting or event.

Click the down-arrow next to the suggested calendar to see all the calendars associated with the accounts set up in Mail and People.

Calendar

1 Click the Start menu and select the Calendar app tile (or All Apps entry)

2 You may be asked to Let Mail and Calendar access your location. This enables Mail and Calendar to select appropriate public holidays and show local weather

3 Calendar opens, usually in the default Monthly view

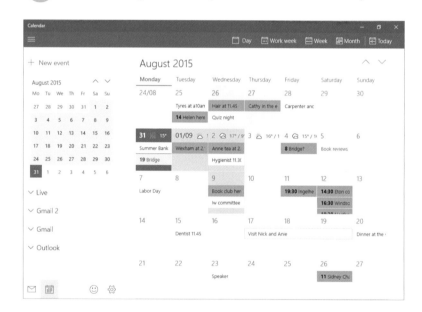

4 Click a day to add an event; either timed or all day

5 Enter the event name and tick All day, or choose start and end times, add the location and any other details, then click Done

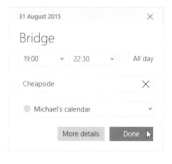

...cont'd

6 Click the Menu button to replace the left hand calendar panel with an icon bar (see previous page)

You can scroll Month view vertically, a month at a time, up and down, using the arrow buttons.

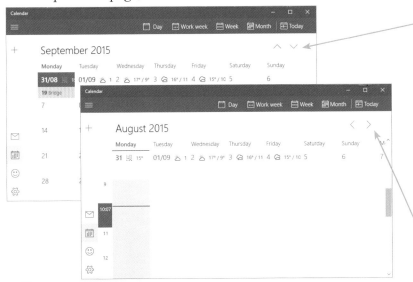

You can scroll Week views horizontally, seven days at a time, or left and right, using the arrow buttons. Use the scroll bar to move vertically through the hours.

7 In the top menu bar, select Week to display seven days at a time (or Work week to display five days, excluding the weekend)

8 Select Day view to see a single day's events

In any of the views, press the Today button to return focus to the current date

You can scroll Day view horizontally, a day at a time, or left and right, using the arrow buttons. Use the scroll bar to move vertically through the hours.

Skype to Stay in Touch

The Skype app offers free video and telephone call facilities as well as being ideal for instant messaging. It is a free app but is not included in the Windows 10 installation package. However, there is a Get Skype app button to make it easy to download and install.

Hot tip

In the Fall Update (see page 231), Microsoft added Universal Messaging, Phone and Video apps on Windows 10 with Skype built-in, which runs across phones, tablets and desktops. However, the initial Skype app for Windows 10 is a Classic app and currently has more functionality.

1 Select Get Skype from the All Apps list

2 Select the option to Download Skype

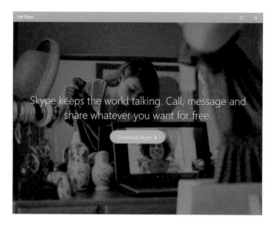

3 When the Skype Setup program finishes downloading, select Run

Don't forget

You'll be given the option to install Skype Click to Call, which can give you free calls to businesses that support Skype access.

4 Follow the prompts to set your language, accept terms, and install Skype on your system

5 Skype is installed ready for sign-in

...cont'd

6 Enter your Microsoft Account email address and password and click Sign in

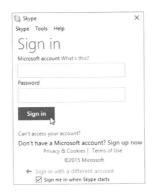

7 You'll be prompted to check that your speakers, microphone and webcam (if applicable) are operational and are given help to set these up if needed

Choose to sign in using your Microsoft Account, unless you already have a Skype username that you'd like to use.

8 When Skype is set up, click Start using Skype, and you can start contacting your friends

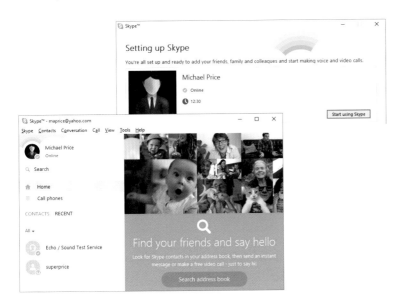

You can search the Skype directory to see if you can locate your friends by name or by email address, and then ask to be connected via Skype.

Windows 10 and Office

Windows 10 systems do not normally include Microsoft Office as an installed option, unless it gets added as an extra by the system supplier. What you do find is an app called Get Office. To see what this provides:

Office 365 is the subscription version, with an annual charge. This product is also available at a one-time charge. It's then known as Office 2016. Both versions include the Outlook 2016 Mail and Calendar application.

1 Select Get Office from the All Apps list

2 You'll see an offer to try Office 365 for a one month free trial – no commitment, and no credit card details required!

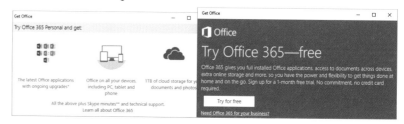

3 Scroll down for the Office 365 Personal trial, which covers all of your devices, and includes Cloud storage

Office Mobile

You may find Office Mobile apps being suggested for your system. You'll find these at the Windows Store if you search for Office. You will find Mobile apps for Word, Excel and PowerPoint, but Mail and Calendar are the familiar apps that are already installed, and there's no such thing as a Mobile app for Outlook 2016.

The Office Mobile apps are available at no charge. However, there are limitations in the functions they are able to provide.

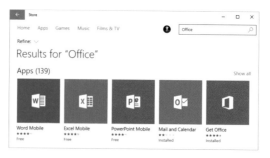

For access to Outlook 2016 you must therefore install either Office 365 or Office 2016 (all editions except Home & Student).

Outlook 2016

With Office 365 or Office 2016 (all editions except Home & Student) installed on your Windows 10 system, you'll have Outlook 2016 as an alternative for email and time management.

1 Select the entry for Outlook 2016 on the All Apps list

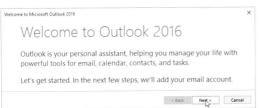

2 Click Next, select Yes to connect Outlook to an email account, then click Next again

3 Specify your name, the email address and the password, then retype the password to confirm

4 Click Next to automatically configure your account

Don't forget

The Microsoft Office 2016 applications may have been pinned to the Start menu on your system, and from here you can then select the Outlook 2016 tile.

Hot tip

If Outlook does not automatically connect to your email account, tick Change account settings, and alter the account type (POP or IMAP), server details, security settings etc.

...cont'd

Hot tip

On the Ribbon, select View, Reading Pane and choose Off rather than Right or Bottom, to avoid inadvertently reading spam or phishing emails.

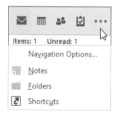

Don't forget

Click the < arrow to collapse the Folder options (or the > arrow to expand it). Click the More Options (...) on Navigation Options for Notes, Folders and Shortcuts.

5 If prompted, re-enter the password for your email account, then click OK

6 Outlook confirms that the account is ready to use and you can either click Add another account or Finish

7 Outlook opens in Mail with the most recent message displayed

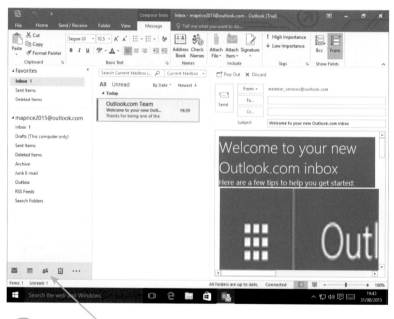

8 There are buttons to switch between the Mail, Calendar, People and Tasks views, as well as More Options (...)

9 Internet

Windows 10 provides two internet browsers to help you navigate through the web – the Universal app Microsoft Edge and the Classic app Internet Explorer. They share many features but offer some unique options, e.g. Web Notes in Microsoft Edge, and RSS Feed subscriptions in Internet Explorer.

Internet Connection

If your computer is connected to your DSL router (usually provided by your internet service provider) via an Ethernet cable, the connections will usually be set up automatically when you install Windows 10, or the first time that you use a computer with Windows 10 pre-installed.

If you have a wireless connection to your router, you'll be asked to provide the network key the first time, but the connection will be automatic thereafter.

To review your network settings:

1 Open Settings, select the Network & Internet group and click Ethernet

2 Select Network and Sharing Center to show your networks

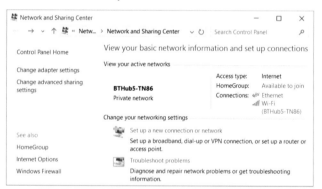

In this example, there are two connections – Ethernet (cable) and Wi-Fi (wireless). Either connection can provide access to the internet. They are both defined as a Private network.

3 Click Change adapter settings (in the left-hand pane in the image in Step 2) to see more details of the connections available

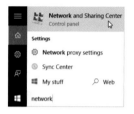

...cont'd

To set up a new internet connection directly from your computer:

1 In the Network and Sharing Center, select the link to Set up a new connection or network

2 Choose Connect to the

Internet to start the wizard which prompts you to select the connection type

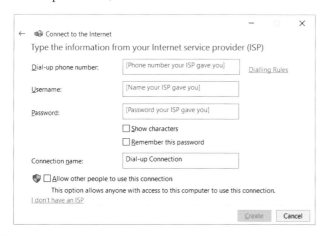

3 Click the type, and then depending on your choice, provide a phone number (dial-up only), username and password, then click Create

Click the box to allow anyone with access to the computer to use the connection. Clear the box to reserve the connection for use with your account only.

If your network wasn't available at the time of installation, you can add a connection later.

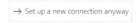

If there's already an internet connection, the wizard will tell you, but will allow you to continue and set up a second connection, for example a dialup backup for your DSL connection.

→ Set up a new connection anyway

Browse the Web

By default, Windows 10 provides access to the internet via Edge: the new browser from Microsoft. Internet Explorer v11.0 is also available, for websites that do not work with Edge.

If you are running Windows 10 in Tablet mode, icons are not normally displayed on the Taskbar, so select the Microsoft Edge tile from the Start menu.

You can also start Microsoft Edge from All Apps.

1 Click the Microsoft Edge icon on the Taskbar to open the app

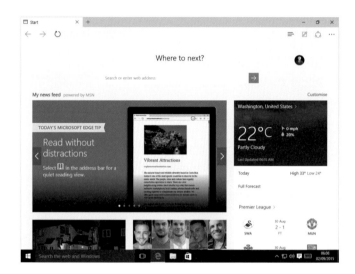

2 The Start screen displays, with a News channel provided by MSN. Scroll down for more items

You can scroll the screen with the mouse wheel, with the scroll bar that appears when you move the mouse, or by dragging the scrollbar on a touch monitor.

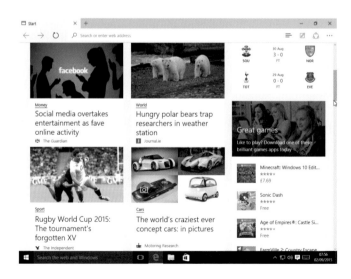

...cont'd

3 Click in the Search box at the top of the Start screen and begin typing, to see related Search suggestions

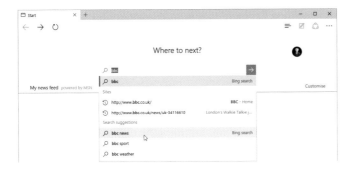

The Hub (see page 166) gives access to the Favorites, Reading List, History and Downloads.

4 Choose one of the Search suggestions to see the list of web pages matching those terms

More Options gives access to a variety of options.

161

5 Select one of the web pages and explore the commands that are available

Back   Forward   Refresh   New Tab   Address bar

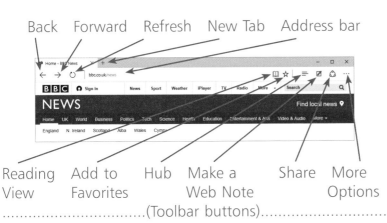

Reading   Add to   Hub   Make a   Share   More
View   Favorites   Web Note   Options
..............................(Toolbar buttons)............................

Reading View

Reading View transforms a web page into a simple format which has less distractions – no sidebars, ads, comments, etc.

1 Below is an example of a web page which has Reading View enabled

2 To enable Reading View, click the Reading View icon (or press Ctrl + Shift + R)

Settings

1 To configure Microsoft Edge, select More Options and then Settings

Choose a Theme
You can have the default Light theme or the Dark theme (see page 164).

Show the Favorites Bar
You can turn on the Favorites bar and add sites there (see page 166).

Open With
There's no Home page but you can choose the Start page (see page 160), a New tab page, Previous pages, or a Specific page or pages.

Open New Tabs With
Choose Top sites and suggested content, Top sites, or A blank page when opening new tabs.

1 Click View advanced settings to review other settings available

You can Import favorites from another browser, including Internet Explorer, plus any other browser you install.

You can clear browsing data that may build up on your system, by selecting Choose what to clear in Settings.

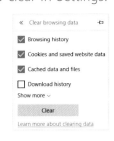

You need to turn on Cortana in System Settings to use Cortana in Microsoft Edge.

Light and Dark Themes

Microsoft Edge offers a choice of two display themes:

You can switch to the high contrast Dark theme if it makes it easier for you to view web pages.

1 Open a web page and the default Light theme will be selected. This is applied to all displayed menus, for example, History, below:

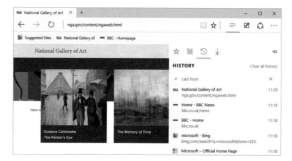

2 Click Settings and then choose the Dark theme

Don't forget

Reading View also offers a choice of font size - Small, Medium (the default), Large and Extra Large.

Reading View (see page 162) offers four styles: the Default, plus Light, Medium and Dark.

1 Select Reading View and choose the Medium style

Web Notes

1 Open a web page that you'd like to annotate and click the New Web Note button

2 The Web Notes toolbar is added, including pen options, text boxes, Save and Share

3 Tap the Pen or Highlighter icons to write or highlight items on the web page, or tap Note to type text

4 Select Save, name your Web Note and Add it to OneNote, your Favorites or a Reading List

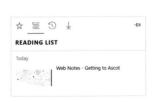

Microsoft Edge lets you take notes, write, draw and highlight directly on web pages as a note that you can save or share.

The tools that are provided include:

Pan

Pen

Highlighter

Eraser

Note

Clip

Double tap the Pen or Highlighter icon to select colors or nib sizes.

The Hub

The Hub is the place where Microsoft Edge keeps all the things you collect on the web.

1 Select Hub from the Toolbar buttons (see page 161) and it opens, initially with Favorites selected

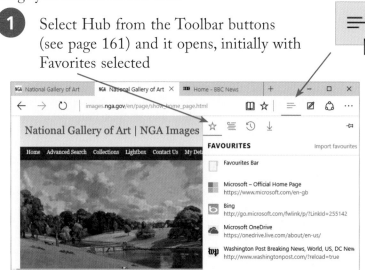

Don't forget

To add a web page to your Favorites list click the Add to favorites button while viewing the page. You can save the page in Favorites or on the Favorites bar, or create a folder to organize your pages.

2 Click Reading List to view the list of pages you have added, plus any Web Notes you have created

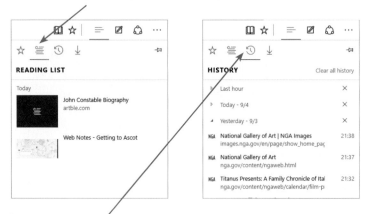

Hot tip

You can also use the Add to favorites button and select Reading List to put the current web page in the Reading List.

3 Select History to see the list of websites and web pages you have visited, organized by time and date

4 Click the white triangle (▷) next to a time or date to see the individual web pages visited during that period (it becomes a black triangle (◢) to show the list is expanded)

...cont'd

5 Click Downloads to view the list of files that you have downloaded in the past

6 The Open folder link will invoke File Explorer to display the Downloads folder for the current user

The Downloads folder is the location where your downloaded files are usually stored, though they may be deleted after use, for example upon program installation.

7 To remove the Hub area, click anywhere outside of it to close it

8 To fix the Hub in view, click the Pin button and it is displayed alongside the web page

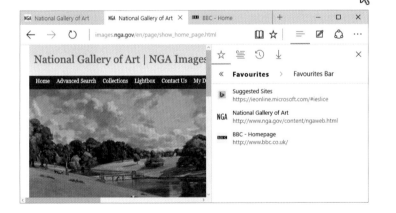

9 When you do want to hide the Hub pane, click the Close button

10 The next time you display the Hub pane, it will open in the area last viewed and it will be unpinned

The Downloads section shows the downloads that were managed through Microsoft Edge. Other browsers may also add files to the Downloads folder.

This shows the Favorites bar, which is a folder within the Favorites.

Right-click Menus

Hot tip

The right-click action is one area where the Microsoft Edge browser performs differently from the Internet Explorer Classic app.

Don't forget

Hyperlinks direct you to other website locations. They can be associated with images, graphics and text.

1 Open a selection of web pages in Microsoft Edge

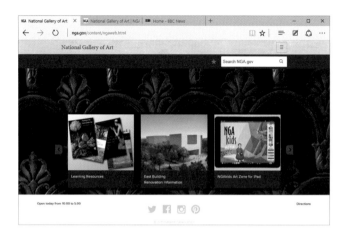

2 Right-click an empty part of the page (the mouse pointer remains as an arrow) to get a basic context menu

3 Right-click an image with a hyperlink (the mouse pointer becomes a hand) and an image-related context menu appears

4 There's a more restricted context menu displayed when you right-click text with a hyperlink (again with a hand pointer)

These right-click actions are quite unlike those you get with the Internet Explorer Classic app. To view the differences:

1 Select one of the tabs (see page 172) in Microsoft Edge

2 Select the More Options button from the Toolbar and choose Open with Internet Explorer

The web page on the current tab in the Universal app Microsoft Edge is displayed in the Classic app Internet Explorer.

Don't forget

Only the active tab from Microsoft Edge is opened initially, though you can add more tabs and switch between web pages as usual.

3 Right-click a plain part of the web page, or one of the hyperlinks and see the various menus that are displayed:

Plain Area · Background Patterned Area · Picture Hyperlink · Text Hyperlink

4 Right-click alongside the tabs, in the clear space between the New tab button and the Home button, to see the menu that controls which parts of Internet Explorer are enabled

Hot tip

Internet Explorer, can display Menu, Favorites, Command and Status bars, and show tabs on a separate row.

Desktop Internet Explorer

1 Select Internet Explorer from All Apps, Windows Accessories

2 Internet Explorer opens in a window on the Home page

The browser icon on the Taskbar opens the Microsoft Edge app, but you can add the icon for Internet Explorer to the Taskbar as well.

Don't forget

Hot tip

Select one bar at a time and it is added and then marked with a tick. Select again to remove the tick and hide the bar. You can also set Show tabs on a separate row.

Address and Search Bar

Tab Bar

New Tab

Mini Toolbar

Back and forward arrows

Search box

Web page content

Text link

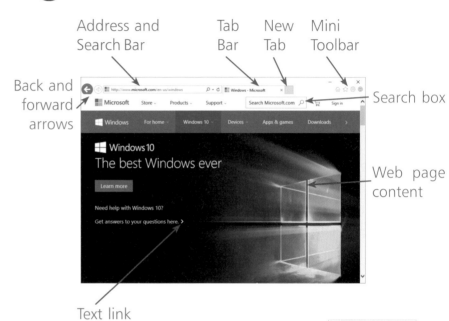

3 Right-click alongside the Tab bar to add another bar, e.g. Favorites

Menu bar
Favourites bar
Command bar
Status bar
Lock the toolbars
Show tabs on a separate row
Restore
Move

Back and Forward
Tab Bar
Menu Bar
Favorites Bar
Command Bar
Status Bar

4 Click in the Address bar and Internet Explorer makes suggestions based on your previous visits

When you move the mouse pointer over a hyperlink and the hand symbol appears, you may see an image description. You'll also see the address the hyperlink points to.

5 Click a hyperlink to switch to that web page

6 Click the Back and Forward buttons to review pages

The web page history associated with the Forward and Back arrows helps you to return to locations you have recently visited.

7 Right-click Back/Forward to view and select from the list of your recent visits

Tabbed Browsing

Using tabbed browsing allows you to explore more websites simultaneously, without losing your place in the website you are currently viewing.

The New Tab button gives you a blank tab where you can enter a URL in the address bar, or redisplay your previously-viewed web pages via History or Favorites.

There are several ways to create a new tab:

1. Click the New Tab button and a new tab is added, and it becomes the active tab

2. Press Ctrl + T and a new tab is added and again becomes the active tab

3. Right-click a hyperlink and select Open in new tab. A tab with the web page is added, but it does not become the active tab.

These keyboard shortcuts apply to both Internet Explorer and Microsoft Edge. When you have web pages open in both browsers:

Don't forget

When you close Internet Explorer, you get the option to close all tabs or just close the current tab.

When you close Microsoft Edge, you must either close all tabs or Cancel.

4. Select Task View on the Taskbar to see each browser with its active tab

5. Move the mouse over the Taskbar browser icons

For Microsoft Edge, there's just one thumbnail for the active tab. Internet Explorer has thumbnails for all of its open tabs.

Zoom Web Page

You may find some web pages difficult to read, especially if you have your monitor set for high resolution. There are several ways to magnify a web page in Internet Explorer:

1 Click the Tools button, select Zoom and choose a level, e.g. 100%

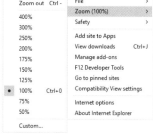

2 Press Ctrl + to Zoom in, 25% more each time

3 Press Ctrl - to Zoom out, 25% less each time

4 Press Ctrl 0 to return to the 100% level

5 Enable the Status bar (see page 170) to display the Zoom button, and click repeatedly to cycle through the levels

Microsoft Edge also provides a Zoom feature. Its methods for zooming the web page include:

1 Select More Options and on the Zoom entry click the + or - buttons to zoom in or out, 25% at a time

2 Press Ctrl + to Zoom in, or Ctrl - to Zoom out, again 25% more each time

3 Press Ctrl 0 to return to 100%

There are no menus of scale factors, and no custom scaling.

Hot tip

Values below 100% are useful as an overview for large web pages. Choose Custom to apply a specific zoom factor. You can specify any value between 10% and 1000%.

Don't forget

Click the down-arrow next to the Internet Explorer Zoom button to display the Zoom menu and select the level required.

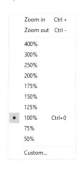

RSS Feeds

Internet Explorer tells you whenever there's a feed available, if you enable the Command bar to see the Feeds icon.

1 If there are no feeds available, the button is grayed

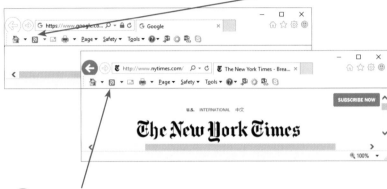

2 When you switch to a web page that has a feed, the Feeds button changes color and a sound may play

3 Click the down-arrow to the side of the Feeds button and select the feed to view the reports it offers

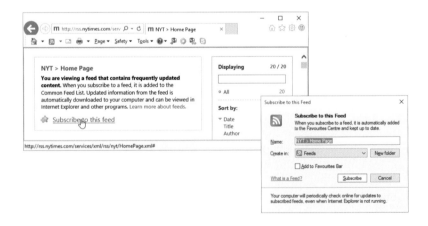

4 If the reports interest you, click Subscribe to this feed, then click Subscribe and you'll be able to view updated content in Internet Explorer or in your Outlook 2016 email app.

10 Windows Games

You can access Xbox Games or the Windows Store, to find a variety of products to challenge and teach. Record your scores and compare your results with friends, or other players.

Games in Windows 10

In previous releases of Windows, a good selection of games were included in the initial installation. In Windows 7, for example, you'd find the following in the Games folder:

Associated with this folder was the Games Explorer, which helped you to get software updates and news feeds for the installed games. The Games Explorer also tracked wins, losses and other statistics.

You won't find these games in Windows 10, since they are not pre-installed, and Microsoft includes only one Universal game app, the Microsoft Solitaire Collection. However, you will find many games available at the Windows Store (see page 128). These include many free games, though you should be aware that there may be in-app purchases being suggested during play.

Microsoft has integrated Xbox content and gaming services into Windows 10, and provides the Xbox app (see page 186). This gives Windows 10 players access to the Xbox Live network, so they can keep track of their achievements, see what their friends are playing and participate in multi-player games. Xbox One users can also stream their Xbox games to their Windows 10 PC.

Games at the Windows Store

1 Open the Windows Store and select Games, to see featured items and games selected for you

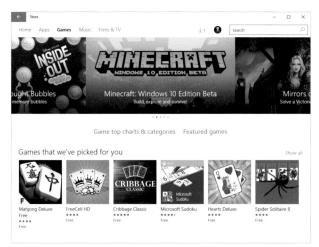

2 Scroll down to see a selection of Top free games

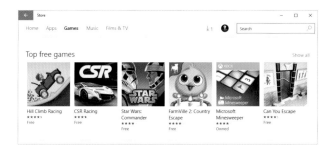

3 Scroll further down to view the Top paid games (shown in no obvious sequence)

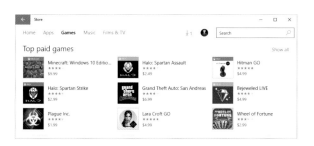

The games that are featured and the games selected for each list will change frequently, but these examples illustrate the type of findings you can expect.

You can scroll the selection horizontally using the arrow boxes that appear as you move the mouse.

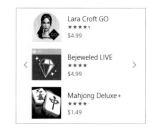

Alternatively, click **Show all** to browse the complete set of games in any of the groups.

...cont'd

4 Scroll on to review the selection of Best-rated games (The vertical Scroll bar appears when you move the mouse over the window, but disappears after a few seconds if you stop moving the mouse. You can also Scroll using the wheel on your mouse.)

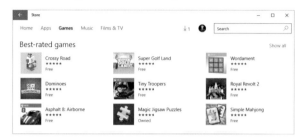

5 You can also view New and rising games, or explore Collections of games

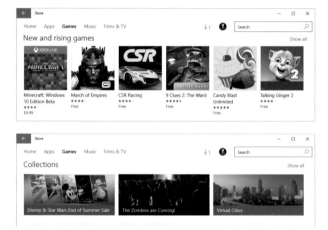

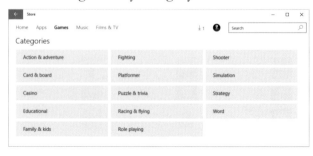
6 Scroll downwards to the bottom of the page and you can select games by category

Word Games

Word Search
★★★★★
Free

1 Go to the Store, and search for games under the term "word search". Our search found 79 such games

2 Select the entry for Word Search and follow the prompts to install it on your system

Free

3 Open Word Search from the All Apps list

Word Search
New

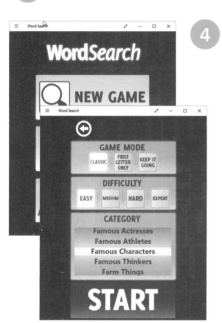

4 Select a game mode, the difficulty level and a category and click Start

5 Locate the words in the panel

6 Even in such a simple game, you can use the mouse, keyboard or touchscreen to select the letters that make up the words

7 When you finish, you are offered the option to specify a player name and to submit your scores online

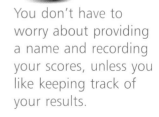

179

Don't forget

You can choose games that are complex and challenging, such as Mahjong and Solitaire, or choose simple games that are easy and fun to play, for example, Word Games.

Hot tip

You don't have to worry about providing a name and recording your scores, unless you like keeping track of your results.

Microsoft Solitaire Collection

1 Find the game in the Store, and note that it is already installed on your system

2 Select the Store entry to see the description

If you have enjoyed playing FreeCell or Spider Solitaire in a previous release of Windows, you'll be pleased to find the Microsoft Solitaire Collection in the Store.

3 You are advised of in-app purchase options

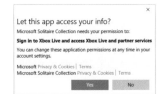

4 Select Open from the Store entry, or select the game's tile on the Start menu

By allowing access, you will have a record of the results for all the games you play and you can share your achievements with other players.

5 The first time, you'll be asked to allow the game to access and update your Xbox Live info

6 The game loads up and offers you the choice of Klondike, Spider, FreeCell, Pyramid and TriPeaks

You will also have access to the Daily Challenges, Awards, Achievements and Statistics.

...cont'd

7 There is a choice of themes for the playing cards, though not all themes will be available initially

8 Select a game, e.g. FreeCell, and it starts with an optional tutorial on how to play the game. Click Next to go through the tutorial or click Close

9 Close the tutorial and begin playing the game

The Theme specifies the card deck style and the play area background for all of the games in the collection.

You'll see links to other Xbox games that are available for Windows 10 devices.

Click the Do not show again box to avoid loading the tutorial when you open the game in future.

Microsoft Minesweeper

Don't forget

The process that you follow to install and play Minesweeper is typical for Xbox games on Windows 10 PCs.

1 Find Microsoft Minesweeper in the Windows Store to view the description (noting the in-app purchases)

2 Click Free and follow the prompts to install the game, and choose to Pin to Start if you wish to add a tile to the Start menu

3 Select the tile, or locate the app from the All Apps list, to open the game

The first time you play, you'll be asked to allow the game to access and update your Xbox Live information if you have an Xbox gamertag.

Hot tip

You could also open the game from the Open button now shown in the Windows Store entry for the game.

4 Choose one of the game types, such as Easy 9x9 to get started, or a more advanced level depending on your ability

...cont'd

5 The game starts, and the first time you play you are offered an optional tutorial with hints and prompts to explain how it works. You can either skip this or go through the tutorial

You use the number displayed to help deduce whether a square is safe to uncover. Right-click a suspect square to add a flag, or left-click a safe cell. On a touchscreen, you would press for a flag or tap for a safe cell.

6 The first click is safe, but after that you must check carefully before selecting a cell as safe or potentially mined

Open the Xbox app (see page 186) and select Achievements from the menu to see the results for the recent games you have played.

7 If you go wrong the results will be explosive, and the game will terminate

8 Get it right, and you are treated to fireworks at the end of the game

9 Your scores are recorded and made available to the Xbox app (assuming you have an Xbox gamertag) so they can be shared with other players

183

Microsoft Mahjong

1 Locate the game in the Store, and click the Free button to install it, then pin it to the Start menu if required

Don't forget

This game has three skill levels, with four puzzles for each, giving 12 in total. It can be played with keyboard, mouse or by touch.

2 Select the Tile for the game (or select the All Apps entry)

3 The first time you play the game, you are asked for permission to access your Xbox Live info, assuming you have an Xbox gamertag

4 Select Choose puzzle

5 You start off with one Easy choice puzzle unlocked

Hot tip

As with all the Xbox Live games, you get a record of your scores for all the puzzles and you can compare your results with other players, if you create an Xbox gamertag.

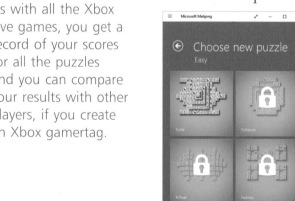

6 Each time you complete a puzzle in a group, the next one will be unlocked and available to play

7 Select the puzzle you want to play (or replay another time)

...cont'd

8   Click matching pairs of free tiles to remove them

9   If you get stuck, press H for a hint and two matching tiles will flash

10   Fireworks are displayed when you complete the game and the next puzzle gets unlocked

11   Click OK, then select Choose puzzle, New game or Share

12   You'll see each of the higher skill levels starts off with one puzzle unlocked and available to play

Don't forget

The first time you play, you are offered a tutorial to help you learn the basic operations of the game. You can Skip the tutorial if you wish.

Hot tip

If there's a particular puzzle you find you like to relax with, you can select it and click Pin to Start.

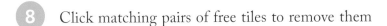

Xbox App

The Xbox app manages scores for Windows 10 versions of Xbox games. You do not have to own an Xbox games device.

1 Click the Xbox tile on the Start menu and the Xbox app will offer to create a gamertag

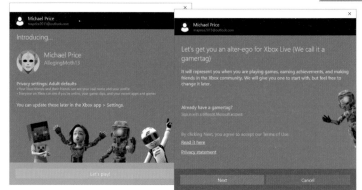

2 The selected gamertag name and image are displayed but you can change these in the Xbox app settings

3 Click Let's play!, and Xbox opens ready for you to add friends or connect with the suggested players

4 Click Store to search for Xbox games (for example). Our search found 26 such games

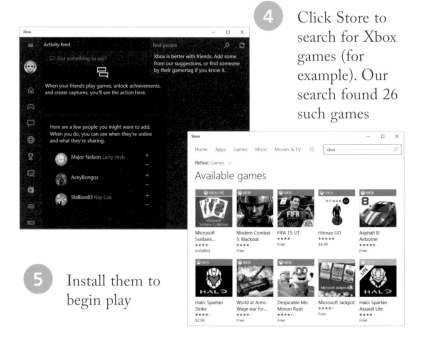

5 Install them to begin play

The first time you run Xbox, you'll be assigned an account associated with your Microsoft Account, and you'll get a gamertag to identify you to other players.

Click the Menu button to add titles to the Icons. Select Achievements to see your results for Xbox games.

11 Music and Pictures

With the integrated sound card in your system, you can create recordings, play CDs and convert tracks to computer files to manage within your music and sound library. You can also manage Film and TV show collections, create albums and slideshows from digital images and photos.

Sound Card and Speakers

The sound card in your computer processes the information from apps such as Groove Music or Cortana and sends audio signals to your computer's speakers.

To review and adjust your sound setup:

1 Select Control Panel from the Start menu, or double-click the Control Panel icon on the Desktop

Control Panel

2 Select Hardware and Sound and then Sound

Hardware and Sound
View devices and printers
Add a device

Sound
Adjust system volume
Change system sounds
Manage audio devices

3 Click the Playback tab, select the entry for Speakers/ Headphones, then click Configure

4 Select your speaker setup, click Test to check the speakers, and then click Next to continue

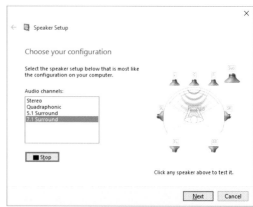

...cont'd

5 Specify which speakers are present in your setup

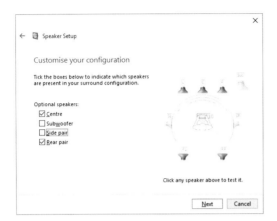

6 Specify if speakers are full-range versus satellite

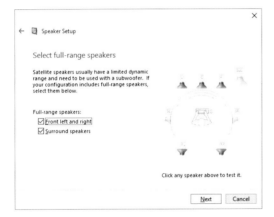

7 Click Finish to complete and apply the new settings to your computer

If you have a laptop or tablet PC with built-in speakers these will normally be stereo and full-range types.

Satellite speakers are external and normally small, discreet and cannot play low frequency sounds. They're usually paired with a subwoofer.

If you have a separate sound adapter, it may be installed with its own audio application programs to set up, configure and test the device features.

Recording

With a sound card in your system, you can make voice recordings from a microphone or other audio sources. To set up your microphone:

In this example, there are two microphones; one a headset and the other a webcam.

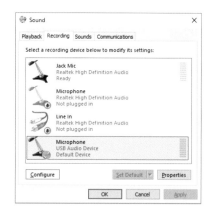

1 From the Control Panel, Sound option, click on the Recording tab

2 Select the Microphone entry, then click Configure

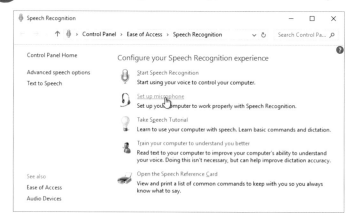

There are several types of microphone in common use, but a headset microphone is the best choice if you are considering the use of voice control.

3 Select Set up microphone and select the type you are using (headset, desktop or other kind)

4 You should set up your microphone according to the recommendations, to ensure clear and effective recordings

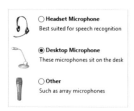

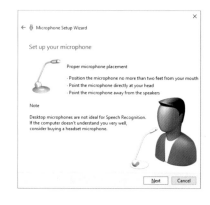

...cont'd

5 Read the sample text and follow the prompts to set up the microphone for the best recording quality

Don't forget

If there are problems with the level of recording, you may be asked to go back and try again, perhaps avoiding background noise.

6 Your microphone is now set up. Click Finish

Hot tip

Repeat the microphone configuration in Step 2 and take the Speech Tutorial, to train your computer to better understand your voice.

191

With the microphone set up, you can now use a program such as Voice Recorder, installed with Windows 10, to record and play audio notes and memos, with the single click of a button.

The recordings you make can be stored on your OneDrive, so you can share them and access them from any computer.

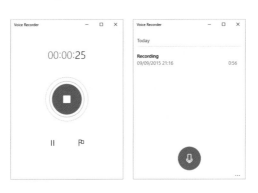

Don't forget

When you've set up your microphone and speakers, you'll be able to use the Cortana Digital Assistant to ask questions and get audio responses.

Play Audio CD

You also use your sound adapter and speakers to play music from a CD or files that you download from the internet.

1 Insert an audio CD and close the drive

2 Windows recognizes the type of disc and prompts you (if a default action isn't yet defined)

DVD RW Drive (F:) Audio CD
Tap to choose what happens with audio CDs.

3 You can choose to Play audio CD (using Windows Media Player) or Take no action, whenever audio CDs are inserted

DVD RW Drive (F:) Audio CD

Choose what to do with audio CDs.

▶ Play audio CD
   Windows Media Player

🚫 Take no action

4 Click Play audio CD. Windows Media Player starts, and the first time you must choose the settings

5 Select Recommended settings, or click Custom settings to review, and if necessary make changes to the Privacy options that are applied

If you accept the recommendations, Windows Media Player becomes the default for music files. Information about the music is downloaded and usage data will be sent to Microsoft if you select the Customer Experience Improvement Program box.

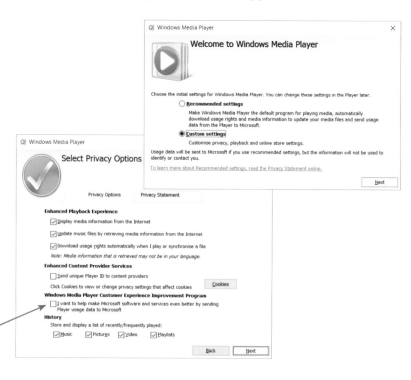

6 Make Windows Media Player the default, or choose the file types that you want it to handle

Windows Media Player is the only option offered for playing CDs. However, to play music files there is also the Groove Music app (see page 196).

7 The CD begins to play in a mini Windows Media Player screen and track data is added

8 Move the mouse over the window and then click the Switch to Library button that appears, to see your Windows Media Player Library, and the CD details

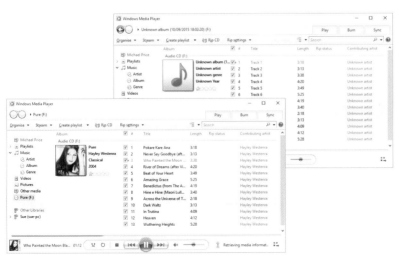

The CD provides the track numbers and the durations, and if you have an internet connection, the CD is identified and the full artist and album details are downloaded.

Copy Tracks

Beware

The higher the bit rate, the better the quality, but the larger the file. As an estimate, a full audio disc is copied at:

Bit rate	Needs
128 Kbps	57 MB
192 Kbps	86 MB
256 Kbps	115 MB
320 Kbps	144 MB

Don't forget

You can choose if you want copy protection on your music, but in any event you must confirm you understand the copyright nature of the material.

 Right-click the Now Playing window, select More Options, then click the Rip Music tab

 For Format, choose the type of audio file (e.g. MP3)

 Choose the Audio Quality (e.g. using bit rate 192 Kbps)

4 Start playing the CD and click the Rip CD button (it becomes Stop rip and then CD Already Ripped)

5 Each track in turn is copied, converted and saved

6 Files will be saved by default in your Music folder, and the CD can play while tracks are being copied

Media Library

The converted tracks will be saved in the specified location, (the Music folder) on your hard drive, in an album under the artist's name.

Type "Windows media" on the Start menu, then press Enter. If you plan to use this often, you can Pin it to the Taskbar or the Start menu (see page 69).

To explore the albums stored on your hard drive and to play tracks from them:

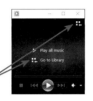

1 Start the Windows Media Player and click the Library button to switch to the Library view

2 You can choose how to display the contents of the Music library, e.g. by Album, by Artist or by Genre

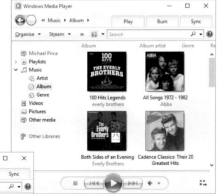

3 Double-click an artist to display their albums, then double-click one of the albums to start it playing

195

Groove Music App

Hot tip

If you just want music on a tablet PC, you might prefer the simplicity of the Groove Music app.

Don't forget

If you run Groove Music windowed rather than full-screen, it has an icon bar. Click the Menu button to see the descriptive names, as shown in full-screen mode.

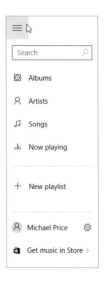

1 Select Groove Music from the Start menu to launch this Universal app

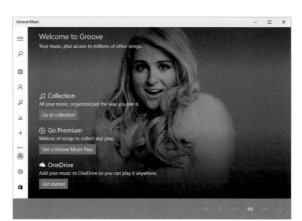

2 You can choose Go to your collection, Get a Groove Music Pass (allowing you to play music from a central server – this is known as streaming) or Get started with OneDrive

3 Select Go to collection, and Groove Music will search on your system to locate music

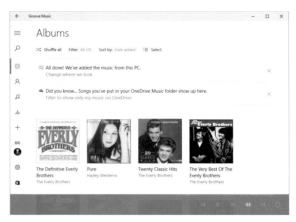

4 All the albums found in the default locations will be displayed. You can review the locations and amend them if desired

5 To search for more music, select Change where
we look

> Build your collection from your local music files
> Right now, we're watching these folders:
>
> Music
> C:\Users\Michael\OneDrive\Music
>
> Music
> C:\Users\Michael\Music
>
> Done

> **Don't forget**
>
> You can click the Add
> button to specify
> another folder that
> contains music, or just
> click Done if you've
> finished reviewing the
> locations.

6 In this case, Groove Music looks at the current user's
Music folders in the Library and on the OneDrive

7 Click Filter to display items that are
Only on this device

> Filter: Only on this device (11)
>
> All
>
> Available offline
>
> Streaming
>
> Only on this device
>
> On OneDrive

> **Don't forget**
>
> You can play albums
> that are on OneDrive
> on any device when
> you sign in with your
> Microsoft Account.

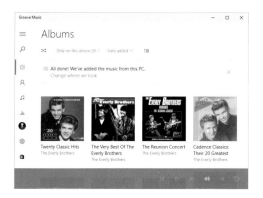

8 Groove Music has
a Dark style, shown
here with the filter
set to show albums
On OneDrive

> **Hot tip**
>
> To change the style of
> Groove Music, select
> Settings and choose
> Dark or Light for the
> Background.

> Background
>
> Light
> Dark

197

Playing Music

1 In the Groove Music app, click the Select button and choose an album and a command bar appears, with a More button if needed

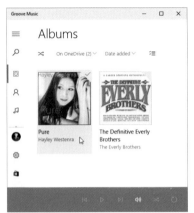

2 Click Play to hear the album, and double-click the album cover to switch to the song list view

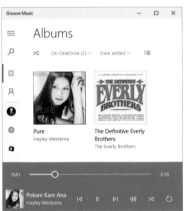
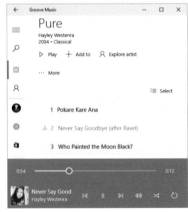

In either view, the Play controls are displayed: drag the play indicator to advance the song or replay, go forward to the next song or back to the previous one, and pause or resume play.

3 Select the Speaker icon and drag the slider to adjust volume

Hot tip

The Play controls also provide Shuffle (to play the songs on the album in random order) and Repeat (to automatically restart the album when it completes playing).

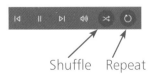

Shuffle Repeat

...cont'd

4 Click the Get music in Store arrow from the menu (see page 196), and the Store opens with the Music tab selected

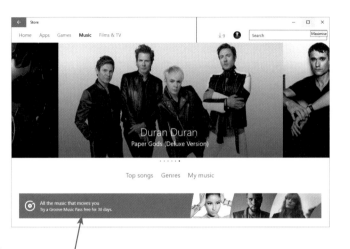

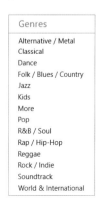

Hot tip

With the Groove Music Pass you have unlimited ad-free streaming, and offline listening on PC, tablet or phone, from a catalog of over 40 million tracks, for a monthly subscription of $9.99.

5 You can review featured artists, and select the information bar to get details of the Groove Music Pass and the 30 day free trial

6 Scroll down to view selections or click Show all to view the New music, Top selling songs, Top albums or Top artists categories

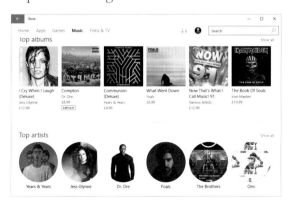

Hot tip

You can also view the available music by genre, with 14 categories defined.

Genres
Alternative / Metal
Classical
Dance
Folk / Blues / Country
Jazz
Kids
More
Pop
R&B / Soul
Rap / Hip-Hop
Reggae
Rock / Indie
Soundtrack
World & International

Film & TV

You can also add film and TV content to your Windows 10 computer or mobile device, in your Videos library, by downloading from YouTube, or purchasing or renting from the Windows Store.

1 Select the Film & TV tile from the Start menu to start the app

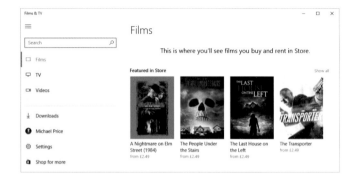

2 The app opens with Films selected, showing any you've obtained from the Windows Store, plus featured films

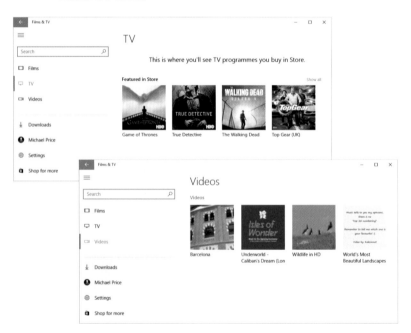

Click Downloads to see if anything is being transferred, to keep your device in sync with your rentals and purchases.

3 Select TV to see any TV shows you've got from the Windows Store, plus those featured at the Windows Store, or select Videos to see those that are in your Videos library

4 Click Settings to set download quality (HD or SD)

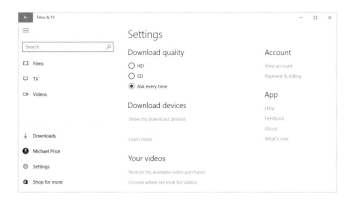

The Films & TV app supports most DRM-free video formats including:

.m4v	.mp4
.mov	.asf
.avi	.wmv
.m2ts	.3g2
.3gp2	.3gpp

5 Select Choose where we look for videos, to specify which libraries or folders the app should search

6 Click the Windows Store icon to get more Films & TV from the Store

Scroll down to see selections of New, Top selling and Featured films and TV programmes, and you can also search for films by Genre.

Digital Pictures

There are a number of ways you can obtain digital pictures:

- Internet (e.g. saving images from art or photography websites)
- Scanner (copies of documents, photographs or slides)
- Digital Camera (photographs and movies)
- Email attachments and faxes

Website pictures will usually be stored as JPEG (.jpg) files, which are compressed to minimize the file size. This preserves the full color range but there is some loss of quality. Some images such as graphic symbols and buttons will use the GIF (.gif) format, which restricts color to 256 shades to minimize the file size. To copy a digital image from a website such as **images.nga.gov**:

Microsoft Edge is used for this example, but you can do the same actions with Internet Explorer, though you do get different menus (see page 168).

You can right-click and save the picture even when only part of it is visible on the screen.

1 Right-click the image, then select Save picture

2 Accept (or amend) the file name, then click Save

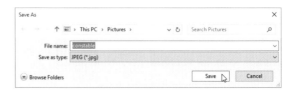

Click Browse Folders to select a folder and create a subfolder, e.g. using artist name, to organize the saved images.

3 To view the saved images, go to the Start menu, click File Explorer, then Pictures, then select the appropriate subfolder

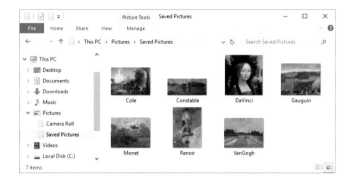

Hot tip

To make more space in the folder, click the Navigation pane button and deselect that box.

4 To explore the folder more easily, select the View tab, then choose Extra large icons and Preview pane

5 Double-click an image to see it in the default picture viewer

6 Right-click the image, select Open with, then choose another app to see the default viewer and other options

Beware

Windows Photo Viewer is offered on systems that have been upgraded to Windows 10 from a previous version of Windows. It is not made available on fresh installs of Windows 10.

Photos App

1 Double-click an image in your Pictures folders and the Photos app opens, showing the selected picture

Click the arrows that appear on the left and right edges, to view other photos in the folder.

Hot tip

Drag the zoomed image to reposition it, and click + or - to zoom in or zoom out.

2 Click the + in the lower-right corner to zoom

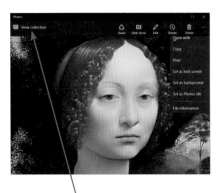

Don't forget

Click the down arrow next to the folder name, to switch between the Pictures library and your OneDrive.

3 Click View Collection to see the contents of the picture folder, arranged in reverse chronological order

4 Click the Albums icon to see any albums that have been automatically created for you

5 Click the Settings button and scroll through the list of options for managing the Photos app

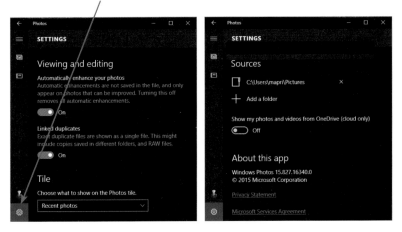

6 You can allow or turn off picture enhancements, and have duplicated files linked and shown as single entries

7 Click the + to add folders that the Photos app selects content from, and click the button to include pictures from your online OneDrive

The Photos app will automatically organize your photographs (by date) into albums of related photos, choosing those it identifies as the best, although you can edit the selection.

Click the X next to a folder to remove it from the Photos app. You'll be asked to confirm, and assured that the folder itself won't be deleted.

Edit Pictures

Open a picture from your collection, and the toolbar across the top offers options to adjust the image.

1   Click the Enhance icon to see the effect (this does not change the original file in any way)

2   Click the Edit icon to access five sets of tools to apply Basic fixes, Filters, and other effects

12 Networking

Create a home network, wired or wireless, to share drives, printers and internet access. Windows 10 computers can create or join a HomeGroup, to share content with other devices on the network.

Create a Network

You have a network when you have several devices that exchange information over a wire or over radio waves (wireless). The simplest network consists of one computer and a router that links to the internet. You can add a second computer, to share internet access and exchange information with the other computer. When the PCs are Windows 10-based, a HomeGroup can help share data.

This sample network map was created in Windows 7. There's no map in Windows 10, but it does show network devices (see page 214).

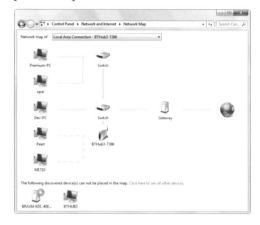

To make connections like these, your system will require components of the following types:

1 Ethernet twisted-pair cables, for the wired portion

2 A router to manage the network connections

3 An internet modem, which may be integrated with the router

4 An adapter for each computer (wired or wireless)

To implement your network, you'll need to carry out actions such as these:

● Install the necessary network adapters
● Establish the internet connection
● Set up the wireless router
● Connect the computers and start Windows

Hot tip

Unlike devices that are attached directly to a computer, the devices on a network operate independently of one another.

Don't forget

Windows 10 detects the presence of a network and will automatically set up the computer to participate in and, for private networks, to create or join a HomeGroup.

Network Classification

1 Install the network adapter (if required) and start up Windows (with no network connection)

2 In the Notification area, the Network icon shows Unavailable

3 Add a cable from adapter to router and the Network icon shows Connected

Windows will detect the network when you start your computer and give it a default classification, but you can override its choice.

4 Click the Network icon, Select Network settings, click Ethernet and select the network connection

5 Turn Find devices and content on for Private networks (home or office), or turn it off for Public networks (e.g. coffee shop, library, airport)

6 For wireless networks, you'd select Network settings, then WiFi, then Advanced options, then turn Find devices and content on or off as above

Often, there will be a network adapter built into your computer. If not, you'll need to install an adapter card or add a USB adapter.

The classification is shown in the Network and Sharing Center (see page 216).

| Network |
| Public network |

| Network |
| Private network |

Network discovery allows you to see other computers and devices on the network and allows other network users to see your computer. Turning network discovery off hides your computer.

Create a HomeGroup

If you set up a Private network and no HomeGroup has yet been established, you are given the option to create one.

If a HomeGroup has already been created on the network, you get the option to join that HomeGroup (see page 213).

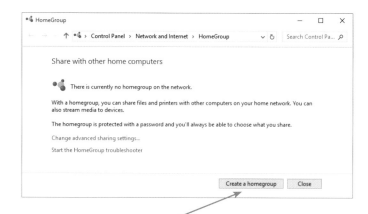

1. To confirm you want to share with other home computers, click Create a homegroup

If the other computers on your network are powered off or hibernating, a new computer might think there is no HomeGroup. In that case, just click Close.

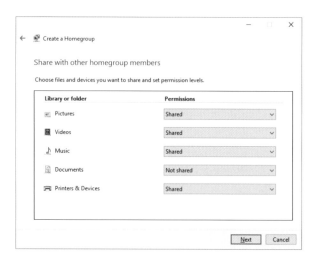

2. Specify what types of data or devices you want to share then click Next

By default, you'll share your Pictures, Music, Videos and Printers, but not your Documents. However, you can change any of these to Shared or Not shared, as desired.

...cont'd

Windows will automatically generate a secure password for the HomeGroup for you to share with other network users.

Windows uses a random combination of lowercase and uppercase letters, and numbers. However, you can change the password to something more easily remembered, if you wish.

3 Make a note of the new password and click Finish

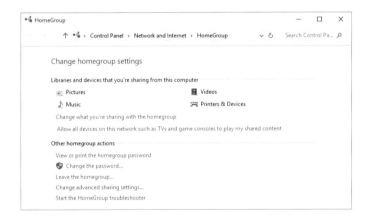

Note the option to allow all devices on the network, including TVs and games consoles, to access your shared content.

4 View the HomeGroup settings and make any changes if required. You can also view or print the password, or change it to a more memorable password

5 Close the HomeGroup Settings and remember to share the password with the other users, in order for them to connect to your HomeGroup

Connect to a Wireless Network

Don't forget

Cabled PCs usually get added automatically. When you bring a new wireless PC into the network, you'll need to set up the connection.

Beware

Your system may detect other wireless networks that are in the vicinity, so make sure to select the correct entry.

Don't forget

Your computer will now always connect to that network when it comes into range. You can have numerous wireless connections defined, for example home, office and an Internet Cafe.

1 Note that the Network icon in the Notification area shows Not connected - Connections are available

2 Click the icon to display the connections and select your main wireless network

3 Click the box to Connect automatically and then Connect

4 Enter the network security key for your wireless network and click Next (or press the Router button to connect without entering the key)

5 Your computer is now shown as connected to the wireless network

6 If necessary, you can change the network type from Public to Private (or vice versa) by selecting Network settings, Wi-Fi, Advanced options, then turn Find devices and content on (or off)

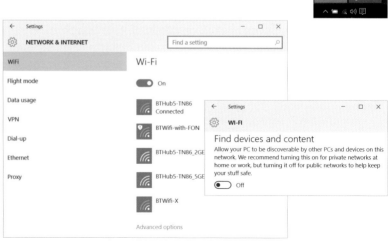

Join the HomeGroup

1 You are invited to join the existing HomeGroup. Click Join now, or click Close if you are not joining, or wish to join at a later date

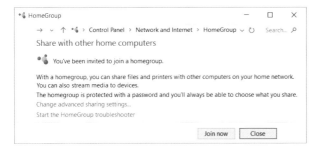

When you connect a new cabled or wireless PC to a Private network, you may be invited to join the HomeGroup.

2 Choose the items you want to share, then click Next

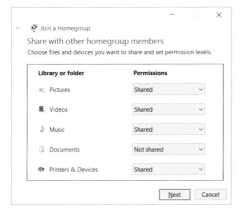

213

Windows may take a few minutes to set up sharing, so you should not shut down the computer until you are told that you have joined the HomeGroup.

3 Type the HomeGroup password, then click Next

4 Click Finish when prompted and you have joined

View Network Devices

There's no network map in Windows 10, unlike Windows 7 (see page 208). However, you can display a list of computers and devices connected and active on the network.

1 Open the Control Panel and click the Network and Internet category

2 Find the Network and Sharing Center entry and select View network computers and devices

3 File Explorer opens at the Network section

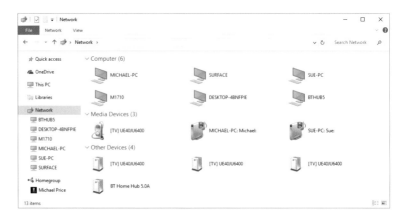

4 Active computers and devices such as hubs, shared media libraries plus internet-connected TVs and recorders are shown

5 If Find devices and content is off, none are found. Click the banner to change, and Turn on network discovery to find your devices

View HomeGroup

1 Open File Explorer and select HomeGroup from the Navigation pane

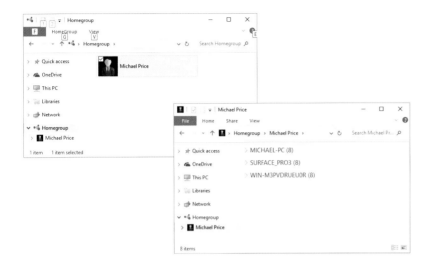

Hot tip

If a computer on the network is powered off or hibernates, its entries are removed. When a computer is powered up, its entries are added. To ensure the display is up to date, right-click in the HomeGroup area, then select Refresh.

2 Double-click the HomeGroup user shown, to see which member computers are currently online

3 Double-click an entry to see what libraries and devices are available for sharing

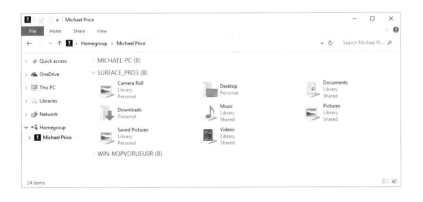

Hot tip

If you initially choose not to create the HomeGroup, you'll see the Ready to create option in the Network and Sharing Center.

4 Double-click a library entry to explore its contents. You can access other users' libraries as easily as if they were your own

Network and Sharing Center

1 In the Search box on the Taskbar, type Network center and select the entry for the Network and Sharing Center

2 Here, you can view the basic information for your active networks

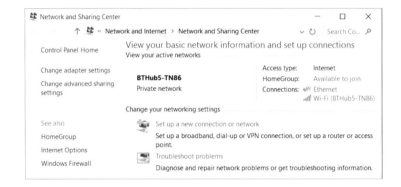

3 Click Change advanced sharing settings, to review the options for Private and for Public networks

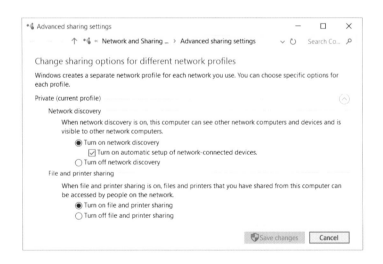

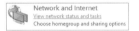
4 Click Save changes or Cancel as appropriate

5 Click HomeGroup in the Network and Sharing Center, to view and change HomeGroup settings

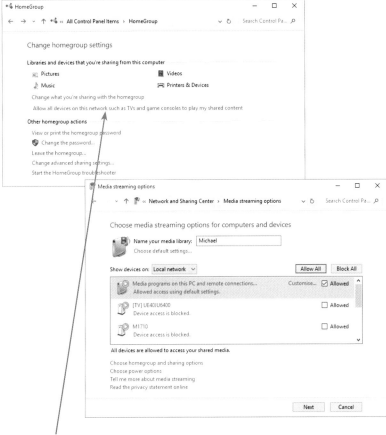

This panel is displayed when you have created or joined a HomeGroup. This link from the Network and Sharing Center allows you to revise your initial settings.

6 Click the Allow all devices on this network... link, to choose media streaming options and click Allow All, to select all devices. Finally, click Allow all computers and media devices to confirm

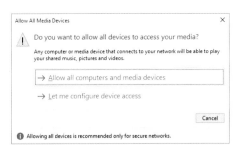

As noted, the option to allow all devices is recommended only for secure networks.

Network Settings

Don't forget

You can also click the Network icon in the Notification area and select Network settings, for Ethernet or WiFi connections.

Hot tip

When you select the WiFi icon, you can enable Flight mode. This turns off wireless devices that you might find on your computer (e.g. WiFi, Mobile broadband and Bluetooth) to prepare your system for airline travel.

① Open Settings from the Start menu or Action Center and select Network & Internet

② Select WiFi or Ethernet, to see the options provided

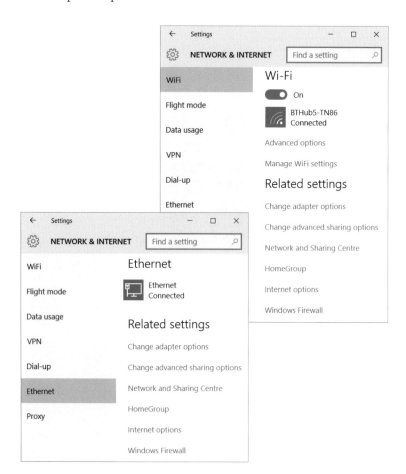

③ From here, you can turn Find devices and content on or off (see page 209), and switch to the Network and Sharing Center and related options

④ You can also select HomeGroup, Internet options and Windows Firewall

13 Security & Maintenance

Help and support is enhanced using the latest online information, as well as many other ways of getting useful advice. Windows Action Center keeps track of your system and a variety of system tools help protect your computer from hazards.

Get Started App

Included with Windows 10 is a Get Started app to help you learn about the operating system, with detailed instructions, slideshows and videos covering a range of the features and functions of Windows 10.

 Select Get Started from the All Apps list and the app opens with a set of topics

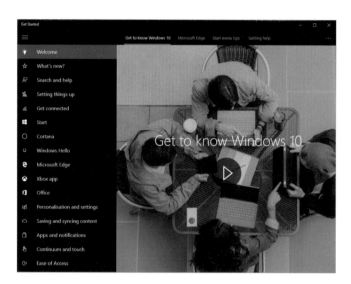

Welcome
This is a video tour of Windows 10 which introduces the Start menu, Live tiles, Installing apps from the Windows Store, Search box, Action Center, Cortana and Microsoft Edge browser etc.

What's New?
This highlights the new features in Windows 10 and how to use them, including Microsoft Edge, Cortana, Start menu, Tablet Pen, Photos app and Windows Hello (sign-in by face recognition or fingerprint) – if supported on your computer.

Don't forget

Windows 10 features a comprehensive set of help facilities including apps, wizards and online support services. Users new to Windows 10 should explore the Get Started app.

Hot tip

You can select the All Apps entry and Pin to Start, and then you can easily access the Get Started tile from the Start menu.

Beware

Most computers lack the features needed to support Windows Hello. Even Microsoft's own Surface Pro 3 is incompatible.

Search and Help

With Search for anything, anywhere, and Search for help, you can enter your search term and get results from your PC, your OneDrive and the web. With Cortana (and a microphone), you can even say what you are looking for, or ask questions and it will set up a relevant Search.

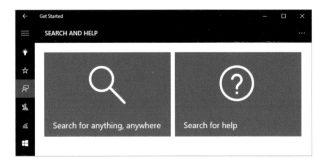

Ask a question such as "What's the weather like?". Cortana will identify your location, read out a summary and display details of the local weather in the Search results (as long as Location Settings are enabled in Settings).

Setting Things Up

Learn about the Settings for your Microsoft Account, your family, your email and calendar and for protecting your PC. Click on any of the settings to get the detailed instructions and guidelines for that area.

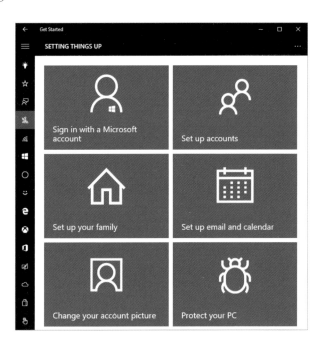

Other topics covered in Get Started include Get connected, the Start menu, Cortana, Windows Hello, the Microsoft Edge browser, the Xbox app, Microsoft Office, Personalization and Ease of Access.

Microsoft Support

If Get Started does not answer your questions, you can review the information offered by Microsoft Support.

Windows 10 doesn't provide the local Help information found in earlier versions, but the Microsoft Support website has extensive help on all Microsoft products.

1 Open **http://support.microsoft.com** and type your search terms, and select one of the results

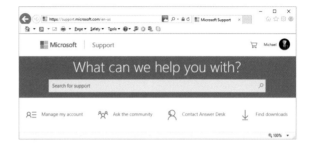

The topics suggested are based on your own setup and include, for example, computers and devices associated with your Microsoft Account.

2 Alternatively, scroll further down the page and select one of the suggested topics, based on your own setup, or choose View all Microsoft products

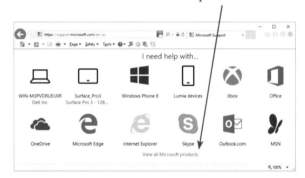

3 Review the options and select the most appropriate, for example click Windows 10

Scroll on further to see other support topic areas, and for links to other useful websites.

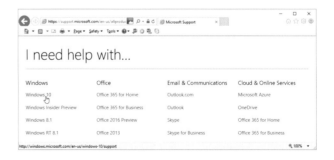

4 Choose from the list of Trending Topics presented, or, if your issue is not listed, scroll down to Categories

Don't forget

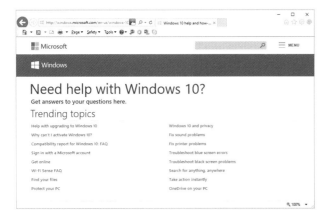

The topics presented will be those the most currently sought after, so you can expect the list to change from time to time.

5 Select the Category that you believe may cover the area that concerns you

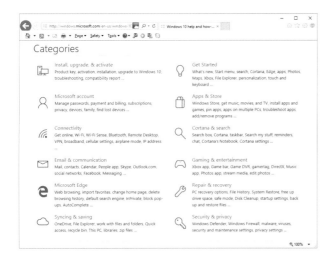

Hot tip

Right-click a topic or category and select Open in new tab or Open in new window, to keep the full list available for further investigations.

6 If you're still unsure, scroll down to Get more support

Contact Support App

If you fail to find the answers you need with the usual help facilities, you can get help using the Contact Support app.

Hot tip

You must be signed in with your Microsoft Account to use the Contact Support app.

1 Select Contact Support from the All Apps list

2 Contact Support offers two main choices:

- Accounts & billing
- Services & apps

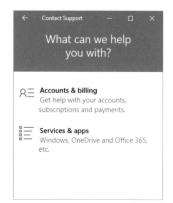

3 Accounts & billing allows you to manage your accounts, subscriptions and payments for a variety of services

Don't forget

Explore all of the topics offered before making your selection, to ensure that you pick the closest match.

4 Services & apps covers Windows, the internet browsers, Microsoft Office, OneDrive, Skype and Xbox

5 If your issue is still not indicated, click See more

...cont'd

There are additional entries for Services & apps, offering more focused choices, e.g. individual Office applications.

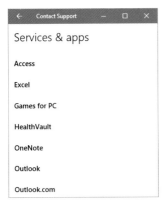

When you select one of these topics, you are usually offered the choice of Setting up or Technical support.

To investigate a topic using Contact Support:

1 Choose your topic, for example Windows, in Services & apps

2 Select the type of help you are seeking – choose Technical support if you feel you need to discuss the issue with someone

3 Alternatively, you can connect with the community of Microsoft users, chat online with an Answer Tech, ask for a call back, or schedule a call at a convenient time

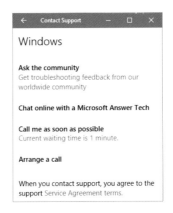

The Answer Tech will resolve basic issues for free, but you may be offered an upgrade to a fee-based service for more complex issues.

Windows Action Center

Messages and warnings from the Windows system and
installed apps are displayed via the Notification area within
the Action Center. To display the Action Center:

1 Swipe in from the right edge, or
click the Action Center icon

2 The Action
Center opens
as a semi-
transparent bar,
with alerts at
the top and
Action buttons
at the bottom

The contents depend
on the particular
system. This figure
shows the entries
displayed in the Action
Center for a Surface
Pro 3 running in
Tablet mode.

Don't
forget

If you are getting too
many alerts, or just
want to avoid possible
interruptions, you can
right-click the icon and
select Turn on quiet
hours (or click the
Quiet hours button on
the Action Center).

Open Action Centre

Turn on quiet hours

3 You can click Collapse
to reduce the number of
buttons to four Quick
Action items, and click
Expand to redisplay all the buttons

4 Select the All settings button, then System, then Notifications & actions, and then review and change your Quick Actions

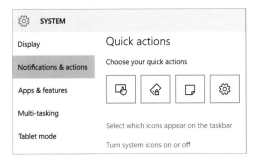

Again, these images are from the Surface Pro 3, so the Quick Actions include Tablet mode, Rotation lock, Note and All settings.

5 Scroll down to select the types of notifications and manage different Notifications settings

227

You can choose to Hide notifications while presenting, to prevent pop-up notifications while you are using PowerPoint or projecting the display to a second screen.

6 Scroll on to select which apps can show notifications

Program Compatibility

1 Open Settings and search for Compatibility, then select Run programs made for previous versions of Windows

2 Click Next to find and fix problems with running older programs in Windows 10

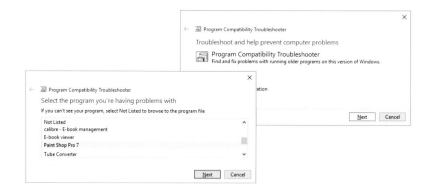

3 Select a program that may have problems, then click Try recommended settings

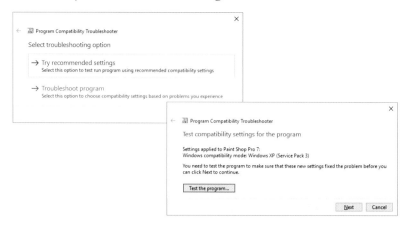

4 Click Test the program to see if the selected settings were successful

Windows Defender

1 Select Settings, Update & Security, Windows Defender and click Use Windows Defender

2 Windows Defender opens to display the computer's latest status

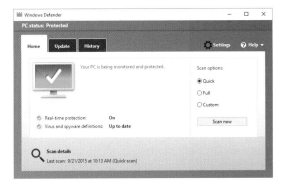

3 Click Scan now and Windows Defender will carry out a quick scan of your computer and report results

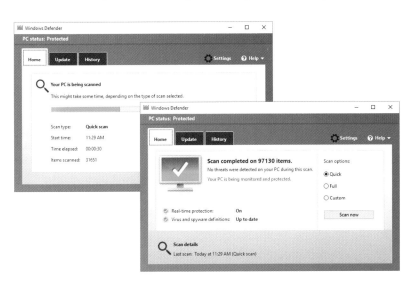

Windows Defender provides protection against malicious software such as viruses and spyware, so you do not have to install separate utilities.

You can also select Windows Defender from the All Apps list on the Start menu.

Windows Defender also alerts you when spyware attempts to install or run, or when programs try to change important Windows settings.

Windows Firewall

To protect your computer from malicious software while it is connected to the internet, you need Firewall software. This is included in Windows 10.

1 Open the Control Panel, select the System and Security category and click Windows Firewall

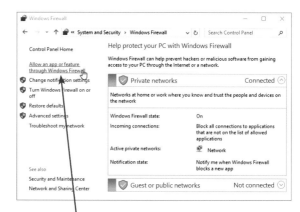

Entries may be added automatically when apps are installed, for example when you download and install the Microsoft Solitaire Collection.

2 Click Allow a program or feature through Windows Firewall, to view the list of allowed programs which can communicate through Windows Firewall

3 Click Change settings to make changes to the Allowed apps and features, and to enable the option to Allow another app to communicate in the same way

Allow another app...

Windows Update

To view the status of Windows Updates on your system:

1 Open Settings, select Update & Security and then click Windows Update

2 Check for updates if you wish, or select Advanced options to see what controls you can apply

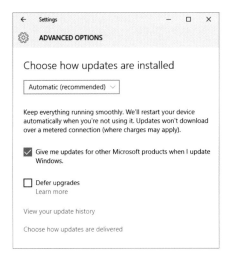

3 If you prefer, clear the first box to avoid getting updates for other Microsoft products, when you update your Windows 10 operating system

This shows that the only real control you have over updates is for Microsoft Office and other Microsoft products.

In Windows 10, Windows Update installs all updates automatically. This includes optional updates and driver updates, as well as security updates and Windows Defender definitions (known viruses and malicious spyware).

Windows Update provided Windows 10 version 1511 in November 2015. If you apply this update, it will include some new apps, such as Skype Video, Messaging, and Phone. These replace the classic Skype app (see pages 152-153).

...cont'd

Don't forget

If you are using a metered connection (where charges may apply) updates won't be downloaded.

Hot tip

Deferring upgrades is designed to make business PCs more stable and allow systems administrators to test new feature updates before they reach their users.

Beware

If you allow Disk Cleanup to remove Windows Update files on your PC to free up space, your PC will no longer be able to participate in peer-to-peer downloads. To access Disk Cleanup, right-click the hard disk in File Explorer and select Properties.

You can choose how Windows installs updates:

4 Click the box to choose between Automatic and Notify to schedule restart

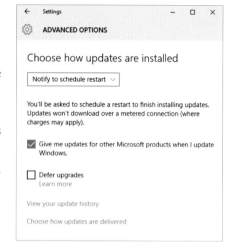

In either case, the updates will be automatically downloaded and installed. It's just the timing of the restart you control.

Defer Upgrades

Professional editions of Windows 10 allow you to choose to defer upgrades. If you enable this, you'll still receive security updates automatically, but Windows Update will put off downloading feature updates for several months until they've been proven in use.

Peer to Peer Downloads

Windows now uses peer-to-peer downloads for updates. For example, if you have several Windows PCs at home, you don't necessarily have to download the same update several times. Instead, the first PC to update would download it and the other PCs could then download it in turn from the initial PC.

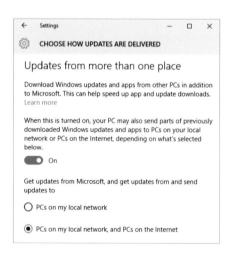

You can restrict this feature to the PCs on your local network, or allow any PC on the internet to access your PC to obtain the update.

Index

D

E

F

X

Y

Z